LITERACY

POWER

- Extreme Experiences
- Communication
- Disasters
- Media & Popular Culture
- Your Future, Your World
- Justice

gagelearning

© **2003 Gage Learning Corporation**
1120 Birchmount Road
Toronto ON M1K 5G4
1-800-668-0671
www.nelson.com

National Library of Canada Cataloguing in Publication Data
Main entry under title:
Literacy power: book G.
ISBN 0-7715-1056-X

1. English language—Textbooks

LB1631.L58 2003 428   C2002-905839-2

Any Web sites visited through www.gagelearning.com have been checked for appropriate content. However, these Web sites and any other suggested links should be periodically checked before the addresses are given to students. Web addresses change constantly. Teachers should locate the URL through a search engine, and check the site for appropriate content.

Care has been taken to trace ownership of copyright material contained in this text. The publishers will gladly take any information that will enable them to rectify any reference or credit in subsequent editions.

Editorial: Sandra Manley, Cathy Zerbst, Nicole Woodrow, Alexa Kudar, Nancy Christoffer, Patrice Peterkin
Permissions: Elizabeth Long
Design: First Image
Cover Photo: Getty Images/Ty Allison

9 10 11 12 WC 15 14 13 12

ISBN-13: 978-0-7715-1056-4
ISBN-10: 0-7715-1056-X

Written, printed, and bound in Canada

Acknowledgements   **2** "Playing With Danger" by Nicole Peterkin © Gage Learning Corporation, 2003. **5-7** "Skiing to the North Pole: Helen Thayer's Polar Adventures" from *True Tales from the Polar Regions* by Henry Billings and Melissa Stone Billings (Austin, TX: Steck-Vaughn, 2000). **17** "Advertising Adentures" © Gage Learning Corporation, 2003. **21-22** "Jacques Villeneuve: Champion Race Car Driver" from *Athletes* by Pat Rediger (© 2000 Weigl Educational Publishers Limited). **30** "Rainbow Man: Self-Profile by George Littlechild," by George Littlechild. Reprinted with permission of the publisher, Children's Book Press, San Francisco, CA. www.childrensbookpress.org. *Just Like Me: Stories and Portraits by Fourteen Artists.* Copyright © 1997 by George Littlechild. **36-38** "A Super Battle" by Diane Robitaille © Gage Learning Corporation, 2003. **42-44** "Travel Challenge!" by James Woodrow © Gage Learning Corporation, 2003. **55-57** "*Titanic* Survivor: Eyewitness to Disaster" by Kate Shaftoe © Gage Learning Corporation, 2003. **62-63** "The World's Worst Earthquakes" © Gage Learning Corporation, 2003. **66-68** "How to Survive an Earthquake" from *the Worst-Case Scenario SurvivorHandbook* by Joshua Piven and David Borgenicht. (San Francisco, CA: Chronicle Books, 1999). Copyright © 1999 by book soup publishing, inc. **72 73** "Mock Disaster Tests Region's Resources" by Leslie Ferenc, Toronto *Star,* Thursday, May 30, 2002. Reprinted with permission – The Toronto Star Syndicate. **78** "The Bridge Came Tumblin' Down" music and lyrics by Tom Connors © 1971 by Crown Vetch Music. Used by permission. **87** "Video Game World" by Oswin Chang. Reprinted with permission of the author. **91-93** "Rock-and-Roll: The First 50 Years" by Judy Jupiter © Gage Learning Corporation, 2003. **109-110** The Federation of Canadian Municipalities, Health Canada, Environment Canada, World Health Organization, CBC News Online, Info Niagara, Sierra Legal Defence Fund. **110** "Average Amount Drunk per Canadian in 2000", adapted from the Statistics Canada publications "Food Consumption in Canada", Part I, Catalogue 32-229, 2001 and "Food Consumption in Canada", Part II, Catalogue 32-230, 2001. *Statistics Canada information is used with the permission of the Minister of Industry, as Minister responsible for Statistics Canada. Information on the availability of the wide range of data from Statistics Canada can be obtained from Statistics Canada's Regional Offices, its World Wide Web site at http://www.statscan.ca, and its toll-free access number 1-800-263-1136.* **118-120** "Life in 2060" by Catherine Rondina © Gage Learning Corporation, 2003. **128-129** "A Country Called Canada" by Gary Lautens. Reprinted with permission from the Estate of Gary Lautens. **136** "Virginie's Story" by Max Paris from *Adbusters* Magazine. **139-140** "Law and Disorder" by Dee-Lynne Scott © Gage Learning Corporation, 2003.

Visual Credits   **2** Getty Images, Inc. **6,7** Helen Thayer. **22, 23** CP Picture Archive. **31** Reprinted with permission of the publisher, Children's Book Press, San Francisco, CA. www.childrensbookpress.org. *Just Like Me: Stories and Portraits by Fourteen Artists.* Copyright © 1997 by George Littlechild. **49** "I should still have all my fingers," artwork courtesy of the Workplace Safety and Insurance Board (WSIB). **56, 58** Illustrations by Ken Marshall © 1988 from EXPLORING THE TITANIC, a Penguin Canada/Madison Press Book. **62** Dr. Oguz C. Celik, SUNY at Buffalo, North Campus Department of Civil Engineering, and Professor Feridun Cili, Istanbul Technical University, Faculty of Architecture, Turkey. **63** AP Photo/Chiaki Tsukumo. **67** AP Photo/Kyodo. **68** AP Photo/Bob Epping **77** Vancouver Public Library, Special Collections, VPL #3041/The Vancouver Sun. **83** "Which Number Are You?" poster by Emily King of Aurora, ON, © Health Canada, 1998. Reproduced with the permission of the Minister of Public Works and Government Services Canada, 2003. **84** "Dream Big Dreams. Small Dreams Have No Magic" originally "Junior Kayi: A Refugee Tells His Story," © United Way. **89** © Zits Partnership. Reprinted with Special Permission of King Features Syndicate. **92** (top) © Henry Diltz 2003; (bottom) © Robert Altman Photography.

Illustrations   **106, 139, 140** Paul McCusker/Eaglewood Studios. **120** Dominic Bugatto/3 in a Box. **143** Tadeusz Majewski/3 in a Box.

LITERACY
POWER

Consulting Team

Breen Bernard, Durham District School Board, ON

Susan Blocker, Thames Valley District School Board, ON

Jo-Ann Carrothers, Hamilton-Wentworth District School Board, ON

Becky Donaldson, Simcoe County District School Board, ON

Lori Farren, School District 6, NB

Marg Frederickson, Burnaby School District 41, BC

Irene Heffel, Edmonton School District No. 7, AB

Ashley Kelly, York Region District School Board, ON

Jinah Kim, York Region District School Board, ON

Diana Knight, Halton District School Board, ON

Toni Kovach, Hamilton-Wentworth Catholic District School Board

Tracy Kowalchuk, Hamilton-Wentworth District School Board, ON

Ted McComb, Durham District School Board, ON

Donna Nicholls, Parkland School Division No. 70, AB

Debra L. Northey, Trillium Lakelands District School Board, ON

Sean O'Toole, Trillium Lakelands District School Board, ON

Benjamin Paré, Burnaby School District 41, BC

Robert Riel, The Winnipeg School Division No. 1, MB

James Stowe, Avalon East School District, NL

Michael Stubitsch, Toronto District School Board, ON

Bill Talbot, Edmonton School District No. 7, AB

Carolyn Van Alstyne, Trillium Lakelands District School Board, ON

Judy Wedeles, Halton District School Board, ON

Peter Yan, Dufferin-Peel Catholic District School Board, ON

Gage Editorial Team

Joe Banel

Diane Robitaille

Catherine Rondina

Chelsea Donaldson

We wish to thank the following teachers and their students for class testing Literacy Power: Sean O'Toole and John Witterick; Carolyn Van Alstyne, Marj Smith, and P. Chester; Amy Mooser; Jo-Ann Carrothers; Deb Northey; D. Brooke Hodgins; James Stowe; Donna Nicholls. Special thanks to Diana Knight and her teachers for their advice and encouragement. Thanks also to those teachers and consultants across Canada who contributed feedback during the development process.

TABLE OF CONTENTS

*indicates Canadian content

DISASTERS

MEDIA AND POPULAR CULTURE

YOUR FUTURE, YOUR WORLD

JUSTICE

ALTERNATE TABLE OF CONTENTS

For Genre/Format see Index on page 154.

Before Reading

Look at the photo. Why do you think people enjoy doing dangerous things? _____

Playing With DANGER

Article *by Nicole Peterkin*

Some people have jobs that involve a lot of danger. For example, firefighters and police officers put themselves in danger every time they respond to an emergency call. That's part of their job. Saving others means endangering themselves.

So why do some people place themselves in danger when they don't have to? Why do some people enjoy skydiving, mountain climbing, bungee jumping off bridges, or taking part in other extreme sports?

Maybe these people are playing with danger for the thrill, the rush of adrenaline that comes with danger and excitement. Maybe they're doing it for the satisfaction of challenging themselves or accomplishing something difficult. Maybe they want to conquer their fear of heights. Maybe they get pleasure from overcoming obstacles.

Have you ever wanted to climb a mountain or jump out of a plane? Is there anything you enjoy doing that someone else would consider dangerous? What are **your** reasons?

GOALS AT A GLANCE

examining reasons • making connections

A UNDERSTANDING THE SELECTION *Examining Reasons*

1. a. The article suggests several reasons why people take part in extreme sports. <u>Underline</u> **three** of those reasons.

   b. Organize the reasons you underlined according to the following criteria:

   Most sensible reason: _____

   Second most sensible reason: _____

   Least sensible reason: _____

2. Look at the photo. Why do you think this person takes part in extreme sports?

   _____

3. Think of at least **two new** reasons for taking part in an extreme sport.

   First reason: _____

   Second reason: _____

B CRITICAL THINKING *Making Connections*

1. What was your first reaction to the photo on page 2?

   _____

   _____

2. Would you ever want to take part in an extreme sport? Why or why not?

   _____

   _____

   _____

3. How do you feel when you are experiencing something dangerous?

   _____

   _____

4. Do you enjoy watching TV shows about extreme sports? Why or why not?

   _____

   _____

   _____

Before Reading
"Skiing to the North Pole"

Skim the title, headings, photos, and **captions** (the writing beside the photos) of this article about Helen Thayer. **Predict** whether or not you think Helen Thayer will survive her polar adventures. Use **one** of the following webs to record your prediction and the reasons for your prediction. You should record at least **three** reasons.

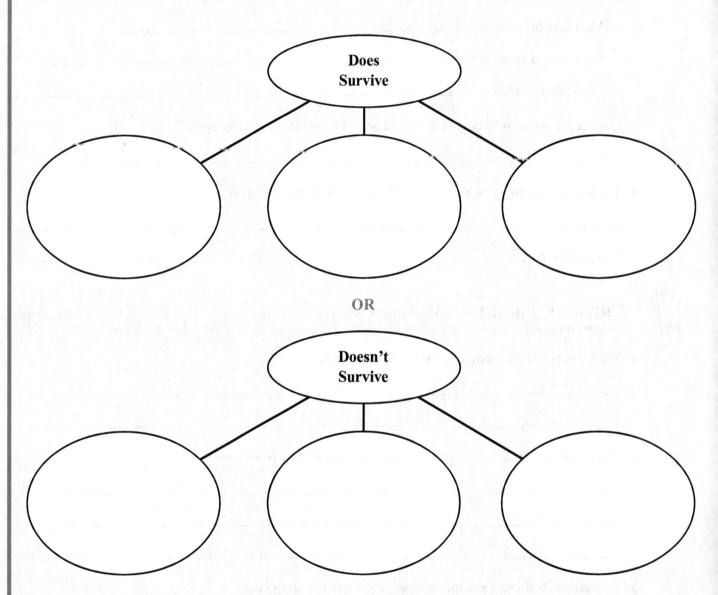

Does Survive

OR

Doesn't Survive

Skimming and Predicting

- To **skim** means to quickly read parts of a text to get a sense of what it will be about. When you skim, you are **not** reading the whole text.
- After skimming, think about what you have found out.
- To **predict** means to make an educated guess about what will happen in a text. Your prediction should be based on what you learned by skimming the text.

Skiing to the North Pole

Helen Thayer's Polar Adventures

Magazine Article *by Henry Billings and Melissa Stone Billings*

MAKING PLANS

All her life, Helen Thayer enjoyed adventure. So in 1988 Helen headed for Resolute Bay, in the Northwest Territories (now Nunavut).

Helen's plan was to ski across ice all the way from Resolute Bay to the North Magnetic Pole, a 585-km journey. The North Magnetic Pole is found among the islands of northern Canada. When a needle on a compass points north, it is pointing to this spot. The magnetic pole is hundreds of kilometres south of Earth's most northern point, the North Pole. Still, blizzards, ice storms, and high winds can strike at any moment.

Helen had planned to travel alone. But the Inuit of northern Canada told her to take along some dogs. Dogs would help scare off polar bears. Many polar bears live along Helen's planned route. These huge animals are known to stalk and kill humans.

Helen chose a four-year-old black dog named Charlie. He was part husky. Helen later said, "If I hadn't taken him with me, I might not be here today."

On March 30, 1988, Helen and Charlie set off. Helen pulled a sled that weighed 65 kg. Charlie walked beside her. He was tied to a chain that hung from her waist.

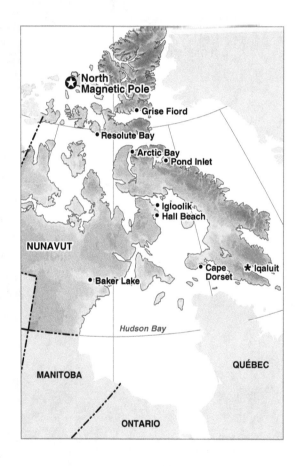

Ask Yourself
Do you still agree with the prediction you made on page 4? Why or why not?

> **GOALS AT A GLANCE**
> locating information • responding personally

Helen and Charlie set off across the ice.

A Brave Dog

The first day, Helen got frostbite on her hands. By the next morning, the skin on her hands was blistered and sore.

Helen struggled to pack up her tent. As she did so, a polar bear moved silently over the white snow toward her. Luckily, Charlie spotted it. He started growling. That got Helen's attention. She grabbed her flare gun. She shot it in the air, hoping to scare the bear away. After seven shots, the animal finally turned and moved off.

Three days later, another polar bear came after Helen. This one could not be scared off so easily. Soon, it was just seven metres away. Quickly, Helen unhooked Charlie from his chain.

"Charlie raced to the bear's leg and hung on," Helen later said. "The bear tried to bite him, but Charlie twisted away. At last, the bear broke away and ran off."

Charlie had saved Helen's life.

Ask Yourself
What information or design elements on these two pages help you confirm your prediction?

More Troubles

As Helen continued, she met other polar bears. Each time she came across one, Charlie did his best to warn her. Still, Helen had some scary moments. One day, she was stalked by a hungry polar bear for four frightening hours. Finally, the animal disappeared.

Another day, a polar bear charged toward Helen. It knocked aside the heavy sled like it was a tiny toothpick. Another attack frightened Helen so badly that tears came to her eyes. In the freezing Arctic air, the tears quickly turned to ice. For a short while, Helen's eyes were frozen shut!

On Day 20 of Helen's journey, a windstorm kicked up without warning. The wind was so strong it knocked Helen off her feet.

When the storm finally ended, Helen stared at her sled. Most of her supplies had been blown away. Almost all her food was gone. The only thing left was a small bag of walnuts. Charlie had lost about half of his food.

Helen still had a week's worth of skiing to go. To make the walnuts last that long, she allowed herself just five a day. Also, she now had only enough water to give herself a half litre a day. Even so, Helen didn't quit.

MEETING HER GOAL

On Day 21, Helen and Charlie reached the North Magnetic Pole. Helen took many pictures and then headed on her way. It was a long way to the place where a plane would pick her up.

On Day 23, Helen was weak from lack of food. She was also terribly thirsty. She tried eating ice, but that just made blood blisters in her mouth.

At last, Helen and Charlie arrived at the pick-up point. Helen radioed for a plane to pick them up. Her head hurt. She was dizzy. She was almost dead from lack of food and water. Still, she had met her goal.

"I knew that I could do it," said Helen happily.

Helen and Charlie stand proudly at the North Magnetic Pole.

MAKING PLANS

1. What did Helen Thayer plan to do? _____

_____

2. Draw a line on the map on page 5, showing where Helen's journey started and where it ended.

A BRAVE DOG

3. How did Helen try to scare away the first bear? _____

_____

_____

4. How did having a dog save Helen's life? _____

_____

_____

MORE TROUBLES

5. What weather conditions did Helen face on her journey? _____

_____

_____

6. What other problems did Helen have? _____

_____

_____

_____

7. How did Helen overcome these problems? _____

_____

_____

8. Return to the prediction you made before reading this article. Was your prediction correct? How did skimming help you make your prediction?

_____

_____

_____

CRITICAL THINKING *Responding Personally*

Use complete sentences to answer the following questions.

1. List **two** facts or events in Helen's story that you find interesting. Explain your choices.

   _____

   _____

   _____

2. In your opinion, what personal characteristics helped Helen complete her journey? Explain.

   _____

   _____

   _____

3. What is the most important characteristic a person who goes on adventures should have? Why?

   _____

   _____

4. **a.** Would you ever consider going on a similar journey? Why or why not?

   _____

   _____

   b. If you answered **yes** to question 4a, explain how you would prepare for such a journey.

   _____

   _____

WRITING *Interview Questions*

1. If you could interview Helen Thayer, what **three** questions would you ask her?

   a. _____

   b. _____

   c. _____

2. Exchange your questions with a partner. Together, discuss possible answers to each other's questions.
3. Discuss why you would ask Helen Thayer these questions.

EXTENDING: With your partner, act out the interview between a reporter and Helen.

> • A **homophone** is a word that sounds the same as another word or words, but it has a different meaning and a different spelling.
>
> EXAMPLES: to, too, two
> there, their, they're
> hour, our

1. Complete each sentence below using the correct homophone.

    a. The dog was tied to a chain that hung from her _____. (waist / waste)

    b. Blizzards and _____ (hi / high) winds can strike at any moment.

    c. Dogs can help scare off a polar _____. (bear / bare)

    d. Helen's planned _____ (route / root) was long and difficult.

    e. She reached the place where the _____ (plain / plane) would land.

    f. There are _____ (to / two / too) huskies in the park.

    g. We will go _____ (two / too / to) Nunavut this summer.

    h. Have you ever been _____? (they're / there / their)

    i. Don't work _____ (to / too / two) hard tonight; you're tired.

    j. Are you staying in _____ (there / they're / their) cottage?

    k. _____ (Their / They're / There) going skiing next weekend.

2. List **three** homophone sets that you find difficult. For example, <u>hi / high</u> is one set.

a.

b.

c.

Homophones
• Look for homophones in your writing.
• Have you used the right word?
• If you're not sure, check the meaning and spelling
  of the word in a dictionary.

- A **prefix** is a part of a word that is added to the beginning of a root word. A prefix changes the meaning of the word.

  EXAMPLE: un + hooked = unhooked (meaning **not hooked**)
  the prefix **un-** can mean **not**

- If you know the meaning of a prefix and the meaning of a root word, you can figure out the meaning of the whole word. Try to work out the meaning of each of the words in the examples below. Then check them yourself by reading what each prefix means.

  EXAMPLES:

Word		Prefix	Meaning
unwilling		un-	not
impatient		im-	not
non-smoker		non-	not
pre-reading		pre-	before
reread		re-	again

1. Use the meaning of the prefix to match up each word with the correct definition.

   Words

   non-stop _____

   imperfect _____

   renew _____

   prepay _____

   unequal _____

   Definitions

   a. make new again

   b. pay beforehand

   c. does not stop

   d. not equal

   e. not perfect

2. Complete each sentence below using the correct prefix from the list above. If you're not sure which prefix to use for "not," check a dictionary. The first one has been done for you. Check that your answer makes sense by reading the sentence to yourself.

   a. When travelling alone, you need to take ___precautions.

   b. He's very _____ happy about the team's losses.

   c. We have _____ cooked all the food for our camping trip next week.

   d. We will _____ fry the beans when we get to camp.

   e. It's a _____-fiction book about polar bears.

   f. She's too _____ mature to go camping alone.

Reading Along

This is a poem about a team of dogs that pulls a sled carrying furs and supplies.
Your teacher will be reading this poem to you. Read along.

THE TRAIN DOGS

Poem *by Pauline Johnson*

Out of the night and the north;
Savage of breed and of bone,
Shaggy and swift comes the yelping band,
Freighters of fur from the voiceless land
That sleeps in the Arctic zone.

Laden with skins from the north,
Beaver and bear and raccoon,
Marten and mink from the polar belts,
Otter and ermine and sable pelts—
The spoils of the hunter's moon.

Out of the night and the north,
Sinewy, fearless and fleet,
Urging the pack through the pathless snow,
The Indian driver, calling low,
Follows with moccasined feet.

Ships of the night and the north,
Freighters on prairies and plains,
Carrying cargoes from field and flood
They scent the trail through their wild red blood,
The wolfish blood in their veins.

**Two Inuit men and their sled
dogs take a break during a
hunting trip in 1925.**

GOALS AT A GLANCE

analysing vocabulary • making inferences

A UNDERSTANDING THE SELECTION *Analysing Vocabulary*

To answer these questions, you can use <u>point form</u> (just a few words giving the main idea).

1. a. List at least **three** words from the poem that you do not know.

_____

_____

b. What strategies can you use to figure out the meaning of the words you don't know?

_____

_____

c. For **three** of the words in question 1a, explain what you think each might mean.

_____

_____

_____

2. a. Circle the words in the poem that describe or tell you what the dogs do.

b. Describe the dogs **in your own words**. Use at least **five** adjectives or adverbs.

_____

_____

3. a. How do you think the poet feels about these dogs?

_____

_____

b. What words in the poem support your answer for question 3a?

_____

_____

Working Out Meaning
- Reread the sentence and think about how the word is used.
- Try to figure out the meaning by looking at the words around your unknown word.
- Think about any similar words you know.
- Look at any root words, prefixes, or suffixes.

B CRITICAL THINKING *Making Inferences*

You can use point form to answer these questions.

1. What work do the train dogs do? _____

2. What type of dog are they? _____

3. What or who is the third **stanza** (grouping of lines in the poem) about? _____

4. The poet compares the dogs to ships in the line "Ships of the night and the north."
   She then compares the dogs to wolves in the line "The wolfish blood in their veins."
   How appropriate do you think each comparison is? Explain.

   Comparison to ships: _____

   _____

   Comparison to wolves: _____

   _____

EXTENDING: On a separate piece of paper, draw an image to represent the dogs in this poem. Either show
how the poet feels about the dogs, or show what she compares them to.

C WRITING *Developing Descriptions*

1. Think about the dogs in "The Train Dogs" and the dog in "Skiing to the North Pole."
   Develop a list of words to describe these dogs.

   _____

   _____

2. Use your words to write about dogs in a format of your choice. You might write a poem,
   song, short story, article, or diary entry.
3. Share your writing with a partner.

TIPS

Developing Effective Descriptions
- Use strong adjectives and adverbs. For example, the <u>fearless</u> dogs ran <u>swiftly</u>.
- Use **sense words** (words that describe how something looks, sounds, feels,
  smells, or tastes). For example, the <u>crackle</u> of flames filled the room. The air
  was heavy with <u>smoke</u>. It hung like a <u>black fog</u> in the air, leaving an <u>ashy taste</u>
  on the tongue and a <u>fine grit</u> on the skin.
- Use **similes** (a phrase that compares one thing to another using **like, than,**
  or **as**). For example, the horse ran <u>like the wind</u>.

- A **suffix** is the part of a word added to the end of a root word to change its meaning.

  EXAMPLE: voice + less = voiceless (meaning without voice)
  the suffix **-less** can mean **without**

- If you know the meaning of a suffix and the meaning of a root word, you can figure out the meaning of the whole word. Try to figure out the meaning of each of the words in the examples below. Then check them yourself by reading what each suffix means.

  EXAMPLES:

Word	Suffix	Meaning
path<u>less</u>	-less	without
joy<u>ful</u>	-ful	full of
freight<u>er</u>	-er	a person or thing that does something
wolf<u>ish</u>	-ish	looks like; having the characteristics of
sinew<u>y</u>	-y	having, full of

1. Use the meaning of the suffix to match up each word with the correct definition.

   Words

   colourless _____

   icy _____

   cattish _____

   trainer _____

   colourful _____

   Definitions

   a. like a cat

   b. someone who trains others

   c. full of colour

   d. without colour

   e. full of ice

2. Complete the following sentences using a suffix from the list above. The first one has been done for you.

   a. The <u>fear ful</u> man hid from the bear.

   b. She was a <u>rest_____</u> person, constantly in motion.

   c. We picked a <u>wind_____</u> day to fly our new kite.

   d. We had a <u>rest_____</u> day relaxing by the pool.

   e. Our <u>teach_____</u> gave us extra homework.

   f. The <u>snow_____</u> hills were perfect for skiing.

   g. The <u>grey_____</u> dog pulled our sled.

   h. The piano <u>play_____</u> entertained us all evening.

   i. That movie seemed very <u>child_____</u>.

   j. The <u>fear_____</u> pilot did stunts for hours.

Before Reading
"Advertising Adventures"

Classified ads in newspapers and magazines are used to sell items and services.
Look over the ads on the next page.

1. What do you notice about the design of the ads?

_____

_____

_____

2. What types of information do you see in the ads?

_____

_____

_____

3. a. Skim the ads. Put a **C** beside the ads created by a company. Put a **P** beside the ads created by a person. How do the company ads differ from the personal ads?

_____

_____

_____

b. Put a checkmark beside the ad that interests you the most. Explain why the ad interests you. Read that ad before the others.

_____

_____

_____

Advertisements

Use these reading strategies whenever you are reading ads.

- Skim the text, looking for the information you want. For example, if you are concerned about the price, you should look for numbers and dollar signs.
- Read the headings to work out the main subject of the ads. For example, <u>Learn to Snowboard</u> tells you the ad is about snowboarding lessons.
- Figure out the meaning of any abbreviations or symbols, such as <u>$</u>, <u>X</u>, or <u>/</u>.

Advertising Adventures

Classified Ads *from* Awesome Adventures Magazine

WEAR EVER WEAR

Canada's #1
outdoor winter clothing and equipment store

- Clothes designed for wherever you want to go
- Equipment to keep you warmer and drier in the nastiest weather
- Backpacks, outdoor wear, survival gear, tents, and more

Visit one of our eleven stores nationwide

Call **1-800-555-1234**

to order our catalogue

FOR SALE   BRAND NEW SKIS
Will trade for crutches! Make me an offer. Shawna, Ottawa: 613-555-8778 Call Mon. to Thurs. after 6 p.m.

WANTED   Travelling Companion Friendly F, 22, seeks same for X-country ski trip through MB and SK. Will follow the Trans Can Trail. Between Jan. 7–21. Experience necessary. Reply to Amy at Box 2458, care of this magazine.

LEARN TO SNOWBOARD
Exp. boarder will teach you all the moves! Championship competitor, risk-taker! Good prices! Call Lois if you dare! AB and BC only 403-555-0023

Snow Dog Inn

20 km north of Jasper
Over 100 km of ski trails

GREAT VIEWS

Comfortable rooms
The best home cooking
Cdn. rates from
$95/night/person

Contact:
1-800-555-SNOW

Climbers Wanted
for Southern BC School of Adventure

- ✪ **Ski trips** from $75 per day
- ✪ **Mountain climbing courses** from $500 per week
- ✪ **Backpacking trips** from $750 per week
- ✪ **Private guiding** from $150 per day

Skiing
Backpacking
Mountain Climbing

Call: 1-888-555-BCSA

GOALS AT A GLANCE

drawing conclusions • making calculations

You can use point form to answer these questions.

1. What is the telephone number for the SnowDog Inn? _____

2. How can you get a catalogue for Wear Ever Wear clothing? _____
   _____

3. **a.** If you wanted to travel with Amy, when would you have to go? _____

   b. Where is Amy planning to travel? _____

4. What **three** advantages does Lois list in her ad for taking snowboarding lessons from her?
   _____
   _____

B CRITICAL THINKING *Drawing Conclusions/Making Calculations*

1. Why does Shawna want to sell her skis? _____
   _____

2. During which season do you think these classified ads were published? How do you know?
   _____
   _____

3. What hobbies or interests would the readers of this magazine have? Why do you think so?
   _____
   _____

4. How much would it cost for two people to stay at the SnowDog Inn for three nights? _____

5. Which vacation with the Southern BC School of Adventure is cheapest?
   a. two people for four days with a guide
   b. one person on a one-week backpacking trip
   c. one person on a one-week mountain climbing course
   d. five people on a two-day ski trip

6. Describe the process you used to answer questions 4 and 5.
   _____
   _____

- Adverbs and adjectives have three degrees of **comparison**: **positive**, **comparative**, and **superlative**.

  EXAMPLES: positive: quick (I am <u>quick</u>.)
  comparative: quicker (She is <u>quicker</u> than I am.)
  superlative: quickest (You are <u>quickest</u> of all.)

  The **comparative form** usually adds **-er** to the end of the word.

  EXAMPLES: fast<u>er</u>, soon<u>er</u>, small<u>er</u>

  The **superlative form** usually adds **-est** to the end of the word.

  EXAMPLES: fast<u>est</u>, soon<u>est</u>, small<u>est</u>

- There are **irregular forms** of comparatives and superlatives.

  EXAMPLES: good – better – best; little – less – least

  There are also adverbs and adjectives that should use **more** and **most** instead of the suffixes **-er** and **-est**.

  EXAMPLES: fun – more fun – most fun (**Not:** fun – funner – funnest)

1. Write the comparative and superlative forms of each word below. The first one has been done for you.

Positive	Comparative	Superlative
a. cold	*colder*	*coldest*
b. great		
c. wet		
d. brave		
e. tall		
f. sad		
g. smart		
h. bright		

2. Many advertisers use comparative and superlative forms to describe their products. In your notebook, rewrite one of the ads in this selection using more comparatives and superlatives.

TIPS

Comparatives and Superlatives

- For some comparatives and superlatives you will need to remember the spelling rules for doubling single consonants or changing the **y** to **i**.
- If you're not sure of the spelling, check in a dictionary.

D VOCABULARY *Abbreviations*

> • Ads often use **abbreviations**. This makes the ads shorter, snappier, and cheaper.
>   EXAMPLE: Cdn. for **Canadian**
> • Some abbreviations you might see in ads are for the days of the week or the months of the year.

1. Write the abbreviations for the days of the week and the months of the year. Remember to use a capital letter at the beginning and a period at the end of these abbreviations.

Days of the Week

a. Monday   _____

b. Tuesday   _____

c. Wednesday _____

d. Thursday   _____

e. Friday   _____

f. Saturday   _____

g. Sunday   _____

Months of the Year

h. January   _____

i. February   _____

j. March   _____

k. April   _____

l. May   _____

m. June   _____

n. July   _____

o. August   _____

p. September _____

q. October   _____

r. November _____

s. December _____

2. Return to the selection to look for abbreviations. Underline all the abbreviations you find. In your notebook, list these abbreviations and the words they represent.

E MEDIA *Classified Ads*

1. Read some of the classified ads in your favourite magazine or newspaper.
2. Using "Advertising Adventures" as a model, write your own classified ad for something you wish to sell.
3. Remember to use abbreviations, comparatives, and superlatives.

During Reading

Read this profile of race car driver Jacques Villeneuve.
In your notebook, list **five** facts you learn about Jacques or race car driving.

Jacques Villeneuve
Champion Race Car Driver

Profile *by Pat Rediger*

Jacques is the son of Gilles Villeneuve, a famous Canadian race car driver. Jacques was born in 1971 in Québec and raised in Monaco. Jacques stopped watching his father race because he was afraid his father would have an accident. Unfortunately, on May 8, 1982, Gilles lost control of his car while driving in the Belgian Grand Prix and died.

Jacques' mother, Joann, did not want her son to be a race car driver. She was afraid for him, so she encouraged Jacques to try other sports. But when he was just fifteen, he attended a driving course at the Jim Russell School in Québec. Jacques soon decided to move to Italy, which has a large car racing industry.

Despite being younger than the other racers, Jacques did well in Italy. He had two second-place finishes and two third-place finishes from 1989 to 1991.

In 1992 Jacques moved to Japan to race and finished second in the Japanese Championships that year. Due to his success, he was invited to race in Le Grand Prix de Trois-Rivières in Québec. This was his first North American race, and he finished in third place.

Ask Yourself
Why does Jacques want to be a racer?

GOALS AT A GLANCE
recalling information • drawing conclusions

rookie: a beginner. To be named Rookie of the Year means you show the most promise.

fire-resistant: able to withstand the action or effect of fire

During the next year, Jacques hired Barry Green as his team manager. Barry worked with Jacques to improve Jacques' driving skills. This led Jacques to have his best year ever. He was named Atlantic Formula Car <u>Rookie</u> of the Year in 1993.

In 1994, Jacques moved to the IndyCar series, which is a very important car race championship. In his first two races, Jacques did not do very well.

Things began to improve for Jacques during the rest of the season. He won his first victory in his fourteenth race. By the end of the year, Jacques finished sixth overall. He was again named the Rookie of the Year.

It was not long before Jacques was a regular winner, including the first race of the 1995 season. Jacques also won the famous Indianapolis 500 race, even though he had a two-lap penalty for not staying behind the track pace car. Jacques set several records that day, including being the first Canadian to win the event, and, at age 24, the youngest. By the end of the 1995 season, he was named the overall champion.

Just before the end of that season, Jacques was invited to race for Team Rothmans-Williams-Renault. This team raced in the Formula One championships, the highest level of car racing in the world. Jacques began to race with his new team in 1996. Jacques did not disappoint his new team. At the end of the year, he finished second overall.

In 1997, Jacques competed against Michael Shumacher to become the overall team leader. By the final race of the season, Jacques was behind Michael by one point.

Michael was leading for most of the last race. On the forty-eighth lap, Jacques tried to pass him. The two cars were neck and neck. Jacques' car spun in the grass. Michael's car glanced off Jacques', but Jacques managed to hold steady. Michael's car went into the gravel and Jacques' stayed on the track. Jacques led the race until the final lap. He was passed by two other drivers. Jacques allowed this to happen because if he tried to speed up, he might not have enough gas to finish the race. Jacques did manage to finish in third place. This gave him enough points to win the overall title. He was the first North American to win the Formula One title in 19 years.

Jacques Villeneuve celebrates his win.

Ask Yourself
What makes Jacques a good racer?

Timeline: Key Events in Jacques' Life

1971 Born to Gilles and Joann Villeneuve

1982 Father, Gilles Villeneuve, dies in car race

1993 Atlantic Formula Rookie of the Year
1994 IndyCar Rookie of the Year
1995 IndyCar champion; first Canadian to win the Indianapolis 500, as well as youngest
1996 Formula One runner-up; named Formula One Rookie of the Year
1997 Formula One world champion

1999 Formula One driver for British American Racing *Standing*: 21st (worst season in career)
2000 Formula One driver for British American Racing *Standing*: 7th
2001 Formula One driver for British American Racing *Standing*: 7th

QUICK FACTS

- A race car goes so fast that gravity is four times stronger than normal. This means it feels like you weigh four times your regular weight, making it difficult to move.

- The more excited you become, the faster your heart beats. Most Formula One drivers have a heartbeat of 185 beats per minute, but Jacques' is only 130 (which means that he stays fairly calm when racing).

- It is very hot inside a race car. Drivers become even hotter because they must wear a helmet, gloves, <u>fire-resistant</u> underwear, and a driving suit to protect them in case of accidents.

Canadian Formula One driver Jacques Villeneuve trains for the Spanish Grand Prix in 1998.

Circle the correct answer for each multiple-choice question.

1. Gilles Villeneuve, Jacques' father, was a
   a. teacher   **b.** race car driver   **c.** accountant   **d.** cook

2. Jacques' first North American race was in
   a. Trois-Rivières, Québec   **b.** Barrie, Ontario
   c. Daytona, Florida   **d.** Pocono, Pennsylvania

3. In his first race in North America, Jacques placed
   a. third   **b.** first   **c.** second   **d.** last

4. Jacques improved his driving skills by
   a. racing in Japan   **b.** taking driving courses
   c. hiring a team manager   **d.** all of the above

5. Race car drivers wear fire-resistant underwear because
   a. it is hot in the car   **b.** an accident might cause the car to burn
   c. driving a race car takes more energy   **d.** none of the above

6. The more excited you become, the
   a. more likely you are to have an accident   **b.** slower your heart beats
   c. faster your heart beats   **d.** more difficult it is to move

7. A race car goes so fast that
   a. it is difficult to move   **b.** gravity is four times stronger than normal
   c. you feel like you weigh more   **d.** all of the above

8. What is the best meaning for the word **champion** as it is used in the title of this profile?
   a. person who speaks out for a cause   **b.** person who wins first place in one race
   c. person who does well in a sport   **d.** brave fighter

9. What is the best meaning for the word **gravity** as it is used in the second point of the Quick Facts section?
   a. force that makes objects move toward each other   **b.** serious behaviour
   c. force causing objects to move toward the centre of the earth   **d.** heaviness

Answering Multiple-Choice Questions
- Read each question or statement carefully.
- Cross out those answers that you immediately identify as wrong.
- Check that your chosen answer is correct by skimming the selection for key words used in the question.
- Reread each multiple-choice question with your chosen answer to make sure that it makes sense.

B CRITICAL THINKING *Drawing Conclusions*

The answers to these questions are <u>not</u> stated in the profile. To answer the questions, think about the information in the profile and draw conclusions using your prior knowledge and understanding.

1. Why was Jacques named "Rookie of the Year" in 1993 and 1994? _____

_____

_____

2. Why do you think Jacques enjoys racing cars? _____

_____

_____

3. Why didn't his mother want Jacques to race cars for a living? _____

_____

_____

4. How is Jacques different from other racers? _____

_____

_____

_____

5. Do you think you would like to be a race car driver? Why or why not? _____

_____

_____

_____

Drawing Conclusions

- To answer a question that asks you to draw a logical conclusion, first think about what the selection **does** tell you about the topic. For example, for question 3, what does this profile tell you about Jacques' mother?
- Then, search for other clues in the selection that will help you draw a logical conclusion or make an educated guess. For example, for question 3, what else are you told about the family? How did Jacques feel when his father died?
- Make connections between the facts and ideas in the selection and your own experiences and understanding.
- Check that your answer makes sense, given what you know from the selection.

DICTIONARY SKILLS *Alphabetical Order*

Arrange the following words in alphabetical order. You may need to look at the second or third letters of some words. The first one has been done for you.

championship   _attended_____

race car   _____

attended   _____

victory   _____

weigh   _____

competed   _____

rookie   _____

overall   _____

drivers   _____

winner   _____

fourteenth   _____

penalty   _____

records   _____

D

VOCABULARY *Word Study*

1. Use a dictionary to look up the meaning of the following words. Write a definition for each word.

   a. championship _____

   b. penalty _____

   c. records _____

   d. victory _____

   e. competed _____

2. In your notebook, write **five** sentences describing a car race. Use each of the words in question 1 at least once.

1. Each speech bubble below has a young adult's thoughts about driving.
With four other students, discuss these ideas, and how you feel about learning to drive.

I can't wait until I turn 16!
I'll get my driver's licence, and
finally, I'll be free!

Lea C., 15

I'll never get my licence!
My family doesn't have a car,
and we live in the city. Plus, it's
way too expensive to take all
those tests and lessons!

Jay L., 17

Cars are way too hard on our
environment. I've got a bike,
and I can use it now. Why bother
getting my driver's licence?

Cathy T., 15

If I get my driver's licence this year,
I'll be able to get a summer job. I'll be
able to drive to school instead of
waiting for the bus.

Andrew S., 16

A driver's licence is like your
ticket into adulthood. Once you
have it, you can go anywhere.

Mike A., 16

My parents want me to learn how
to drive, so that I can do all these
errands, and drive my little sister and
brother around. But if I learn how to
drive, I want to do my own stuff;
I want to drive around with my friends.

Jasmine P., 17

_____

2. In the blank bubble, add your own thoughts about driving.

Group Discussion
• Listen to what others are saying.
• Wait for your turn to speak.
• Stay on topic when you are speaking.

SELF-ASSESSMENT *Reading Strategies*

1. Choose **one** point below. In your notebook, explain what you learned about this skill or strategy.
   - ❏ skimming titles, photos, and captions
   - ❏ making predictions
   - ❏ reading ads
   - ❏ working out the meaning of words using prefixes or suffixes
   - ❏ working out the meaning of words by thinking about how the word is used
   - ❏ drawing conclusions about what you've read

2. Reflect on the selections you have read during this unit. In your notebook, describe at least **two** reading strategies that helped you read or understand a selection. Begin a list of reading strategies that can help you read and understand other selections.

3. Set a personal goal for improving your use of the above reading strategies. Explain what you will do.

   _____

   _____

PROJECT IDEA *Creating an Extreme Experiences Unit*

Create your own Extreme Experiences unit by gathering selections.

Step 1. Think about the selections you read or viewed in the *Extreme Experiences* unit. Collect similar selections about extreme experiences by searching your classroom, library, and at home. Here are some items to look for:
   - ❏ a photo of someone enjoying an extreme sport
   - ❏ an article about an Arctic adventure
   - ❏ an interesting "Quick Fact" about polar bears
   - ❏ a classified ad that is selling extreme sports equipment
   - ❏ a photo of someone skiing or snowboarding
   - ❏ a profile of a race car driver
   - ❏ a photo of a race car driver
   - ❏ an article, poem, or story about extreme sports

Step 2. Skim each print item you find and make a note saying what it's about. Create a caption for each of your photos.

Step 3. Tell a partner about the most interesting item. Listen while your partner talks about his or her most interesting item.

Step 4. With your partner, choose at least **four** selections you would recommend for a unit on extreme experiences. Write a note explaining why you would include each one.

EXTENDING: Work with a small group to create an Extreme Experiences book. Organize all your selections. Create a cover and a table of contents.

When you are <u>skimming</u> a selection, you are <u>not</u> reading the whole text. <u>Skimming</u> means to read parts of the text quickly to get a sense of what it will be about, or to get specific information.

Title

Ask Yourself: What do the title and subtitle tell me about the selection?

By-line

Ask Yourself: Have I read this sort of format (poem, profile, article, and so on) before? What do I expect when I read this format? What strategies should I use?

Headings

Ask Yourself: What can I learn about the subject of the selection from the headings? How is the selection organized? In what section can I find the information I want?

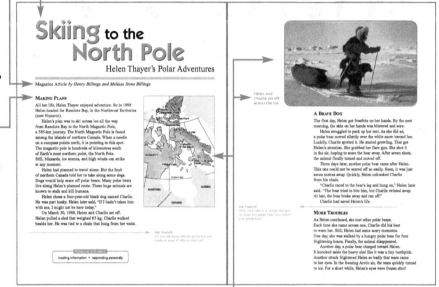

Photos, images, or captions (including charts and maps)

Ask Yourself: What can I learn from the photos, images, or captions?

Making a Prediction

After you have skimmed a text, make a **prediction** about the selection. You might make a prediction about the topic of the selection or about what happens in the selection. When you make predictions, you are combining all the information you get from skimming the selection with your knowledge or personal experiences. You are drawing conclusions based on this information and your understanding.

Setting Goals

How good are you at skimming and predicting? What can you do to improve your use of these strategies? Set **two** personal goals for using these strategies.

Before Reading

George Littlechild is an artist. His life and work have been shaped by his experiences as a child and as a young man. The way people respond to Littlechild's looks (or features) have made him think of himself as a "rainbow man."

What do the words "rainbow man" suggest to you?

Rainbow Man

Self-Profile *by George Littlechild*

VOCABULARY

exotic-looking: unusual-looking in a fascinating way

self-portrait: an image of the artist done by the artist himself or herself

printmaker: someone who uses a press to create several copies (or prints) of one piece of art

mixed-media artist: someone who uses many materials to create art; for example, video clips, trash, newspapers, or magazines

When I was a boy, people knew I was Indian (or First Nations, as we say in Canada), because I had the features of my Indian mother.

As I got older, people were not sure anymore. "You sure are exotic-looking," they told me. "Are you Spanish? Italian? Portuguese?"

I was looking more like my white father. Both my parents were dead and I was living with my Dutch foster family. I was very confused about who I was.

Sometimes I look Indian now, but sometimes I do not. My looks change according to my mood. That is why I have made these four different self-portraits.

It took me many years to accept my features. Then one day I decided that I had to love myself just the way I am. I am a rainbow man, with a half of this and quarter of that, and a dash of a mixture of everything!

GOALS AT A GLANCE

recalling details • drawing conclusions

Above are George Littlechild's self-portraits.

Littlechild is a well-known painter, <u>printmaker</u>, and <u>mixed-media artist</u>. His artwork is seen in galleries and museums around the world.

Littlechild is a member of the Plains Cree Nation. He was born in Edmonton, Alberta, in 1958, and now lives in Vancouver, British Columbia.

To answer these questions, read the self-profile and caption, and examine the self-portraits.

1. George Littlechild is
   a. Spanish
   b. a member of the Plains Cree Nation
   c. Italian
   d. Portuguese

2. Littlechild is a
   a. painter, actor, and writer
   b. painter, printmaker, and mixed-media artist
   c. poet, painter, and mixed-media artist
   d. photographer, poet, and printmaker

3. Littlechild created four different self-portraits because
   a. he wanted to show his different artistic styles
   b. he wanted to make more money
   c. he wanted to show how his looks change according to his mood
   d. he wanted to show off different clothes

4. After many years, Littlechild finally accepts his _____ .

5. Littlechild calls himself a "rainbow man" because he _____

   _____

   _____ .

6. How would you describe the image on page 31?
   a. a work of mixed-media
   b. a painting
   c. a print
   d. none of the above

   Explain your answer for question 6. _____

   _____

   _____

Answering Questions
- As you read a question, note any key words such as **self-portrait** or **rainbow man**.
- Locate the answer to the question by looking for those key words in the selection.
- Use a highlighter to mark key words, phrases, and answers.

CRITICAL THINKING *Drawing Conclusions*

1. Why do people think Littlechild is "exotic-looking"?

_____

_____

_____

_____

2. How would **you** feel if someone called you "exotic-looking"? Why would you feel that way?

_____

_____

_____

_____

3. What is Littlechild confused about?

_____

_____

_____

_____

4. Explain how Littlechild's art helps him communicate who he is to others. In your answer, refer specifically to the image on page 31.

_____

_____

_____

_____

5. How do people usually communicate who they are to others? List at least **three** ways using point form.

   a. _____

   b. _____

   c. _____

EXTENDING: Create a piece of art that explains who you are. You could use paint, charcoal, pastels, photography, clay, or mixed media.

1. Complete the following web:

Who I Am!

Name _____

Age _____

Birthday _____

Home town _____

Important People in My Life

Major Events in My Life

Who Am I? (List at least **four** details about your character.)

---

2. Use this web to help you write a short profile about yourself. The Tips box below also includes some good ideas for writing a self-profile.
3. Draw a picture of yourself, or include a photo.
4. Share your self-profile with a partner.

TIPS

Self-Profile

- For the important people and major events you identify in your web, explain why these events or people were special, and how they influenced you.
- Use the first-person point of view (I, me).
- Use the past tense (I was born… My parents lived…) for past events.

LANGUAGE CONVENTIONS *Analysing Nouns*

- **Nouns** are words that refer to a person, place, thing, or quality.
   EXAMPLES: father, George Littlechild, Canada, features, love

- When you write, try to use as specific and precise a noun as possible. For example, **people** is a general noun, but **neighbours** or **family** is more specific.
   EXAMPLES: <u>People</u> thought I looked exotic.
        My <u>neighbours</u> thought I looked exotic.

1. <u>Underline</u> each noun in the sentences below. The first sentence has been done for you.

    a. <u>George Littlechild</u> sometimes looked like his <u>father</u>.

    b. He is a painter.

    c. He had the features of his mother.

    d. His looks changed over the years.

2. Unscramble the nouns in brackets below to complete each sentence.

    a. I am a rainbow _____ (nam).

    b. It took me many _____ (syera) to accept my features.

    c. _____ (Lichdlttlei) is a painter, printmaker,

    and mixed-media artist.

    d. I had the _____ (eafurtes) of my mother.

    e. My _____ (skool) change according to my mood.

    f. As I got older, _____ (epeolp) were not sure anymore.

    g. George was born in _____ (Emodnnot), Alberta.

3. Write **five** sentences that describe **you**, using specific and precise nouns. <u>Underline</u> the nouns you have used.

    a. _____

    b. _____

    c. _____

    d. _____

    e. _____

During Reading

You are about to read several e-mails that tell a story.
After you read each e-mail, think about how it develops the story.

A Super Battle

An E-Mail Story *by Diane Robitaille*

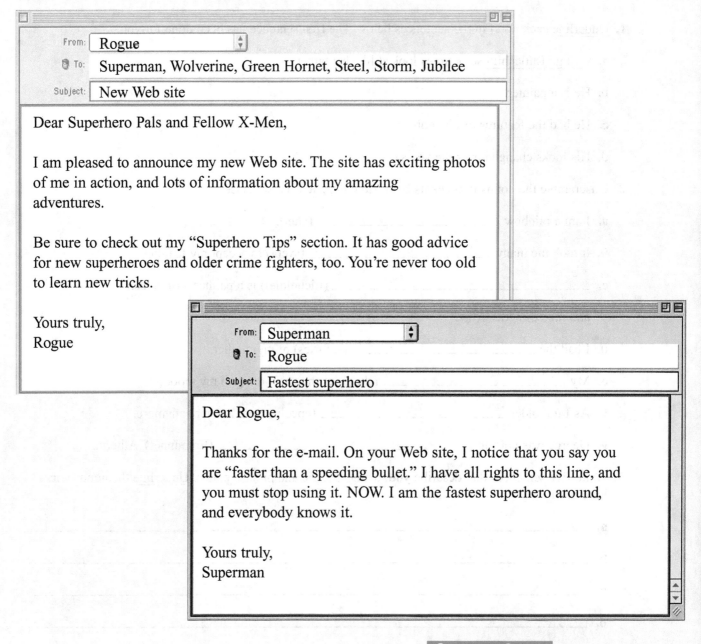

From: Rogue
To: Superman, Wolverine, Green Hornet, Steel, Storm, Jubilee
Subject: New Web site

Dear Superhero Pals and Fellow X-Men,

I am pleased to announce my new Web site. The site has exciting photos of me in action, and lots of information about my amazing adventures.

Be sure to check out my "Superhero Tips" section. It has good advice for new superheroes and older crime fighters, too. You're never too old to learn new tricks.

Yours truly,
Rogue

From: Superman
To: Rogue
Subject: Fastest superhero

Dear Rogue,

Thanks for the e-mail. On your Web site, I notice that you say you are "faster than a speeding bullet." I have all rights to this line, and you must stop using it. NOW. I am the fastest superhero around, and everybody knows it.

Yours truly,
Superman

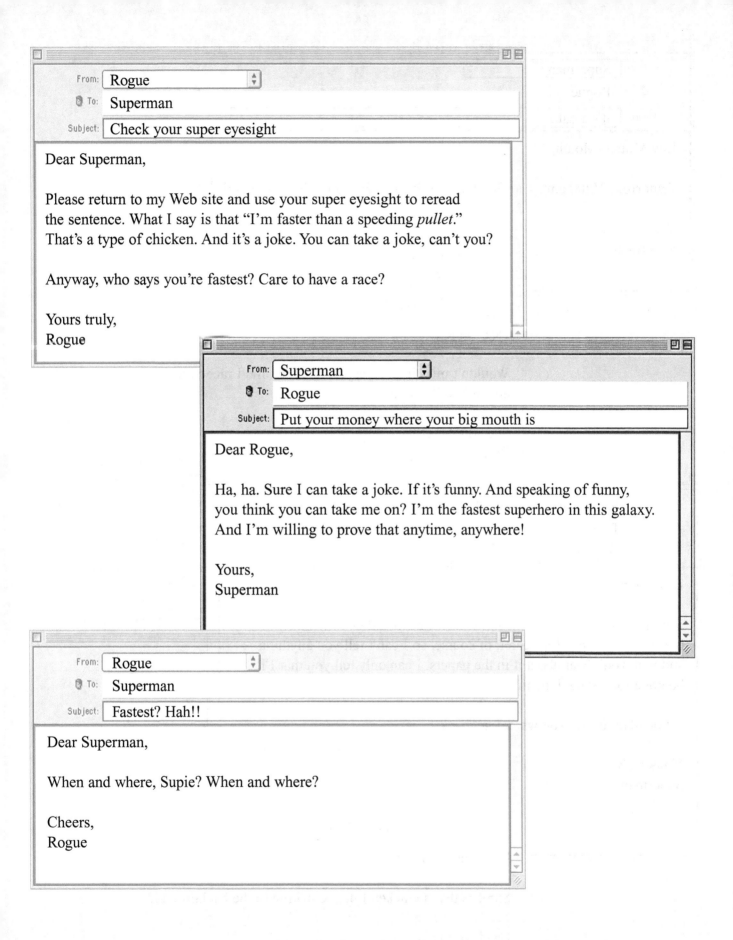

From: Rogue

To: Superman

Subject: Check your super eyesight

Dear Superman,

Please return to my Web site and use your super eyesight to reread the sentence. What I say is that "I'm faster than a speeding *pullet*." That's a type of chicken. And it's a joke. You can take a joke, can't you?

Anyway, who says you're fastest? Care to have a race?

Yours truly,
Rogue

From: Superman

To: Rogue

Subject: Put your money where your big mouth is

Dear Rogue,

Ha, ha. Sure I can take a joke. If it's funny. And speaking of funny, you think you can take me on? I'm the fastest superhero in this galaxy. And I'm willing to prove that anytime, anywhere!

Yours,
Superman

From: Rogue

To: Superman

Subject: Fastest? Hah!!

Dear Superman,

When and where, Supie? When and where?

Cheers,
Rogue

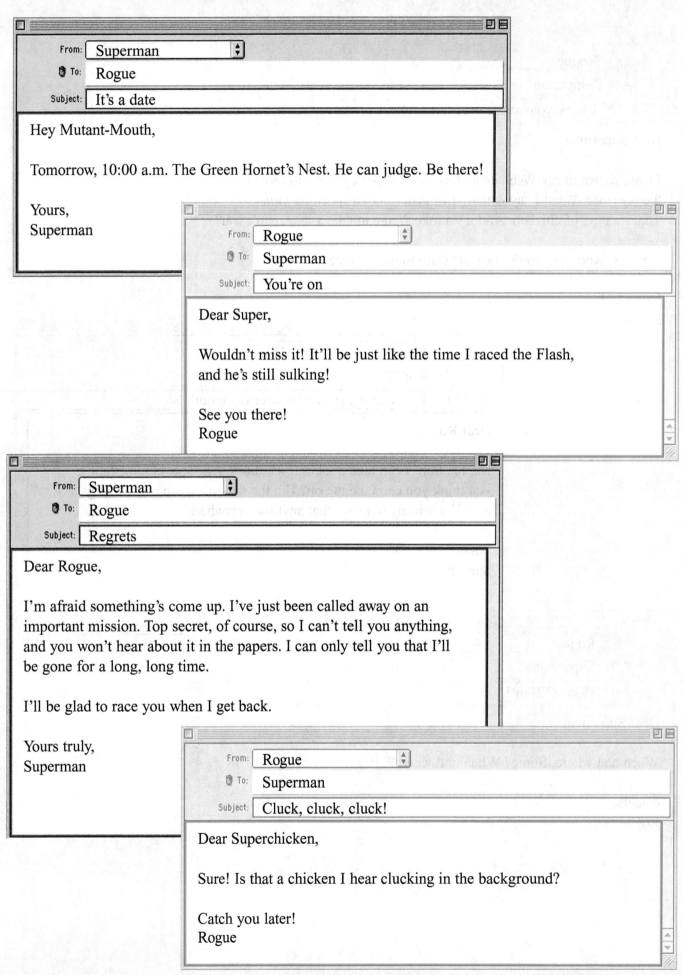

From: Superman
To: Rogue
Subject: It's a date

Hey Mutant-Mouth,

Tomorrow, 10:00 a.m. The Green Hornet's Nest. He can judge. Be there!

Yours,
Superman

From: Rogue
To: Superman
Subject: You're on

Dear Super,

Wouldn't miss it! It'll be just like the time I raced the Flash, and he's still sulking!

See you there!
Rogue

From: Superman
To: Rogue
Subject: Regrets

Dear Rogue,

I'm afraid something's come up. I've just been called away on an important mission. Top secret, of course, so I can't tell you anything, and you won't hear about it in the papers. I can only tell you that I'll be gone for a long, long time.

I'll be glad to race you when I get back.

Yours truly,
Superman

From: Rogue
To: Superman
Subject: Cluck, cluck, cluck!

Dear Superchicken,

Sure! Is that a chicken I hear clucking in the background?

Catch you later!
Rogue

UNDERSTANDING THE SELECTION *Recalling Details*

1. Why does Rogue send her **first** e-mail? _____

_____

2. What does Superman object to on Rogue's Web site? _____

_____

3. A **pullet** is
   a. a type of gun **b**. a type of chicken **c.** a superhero **d**. a bullet

4. Rogue has already beaten _____ in a race.

5. What reason does Superman give for putting off the race? _____

_____

CRITICAL THINKING *Making Inferences*

1. Why might the "older" superheroes find Rogue's **first** e-mail insulting?_____

_____

2. Superman does not want to race Rogue because _____

_____ .

3. In her **last** e-mail, Rogue asks if there is a chicken clucking in the background because she thinks

_____ .

4. **a.** Explain how Rogue feels in her **first** e-mail. _____

_____

_____

   b. Explain how Rogue feels in her **last** e-mail. _____

_____

_____

   c. In each e-mail, circle the words or punctuation marks that reveal Rogue's feelings.

_____

_____

C WRITING *E-Mail Messages*

1. Imagine that the race between Superman and Rogue has taken place.
2. Write an e-mail conversation between Rogue and Superman about the race.
3. Explain who won and how both superheroes feel. Write at least **two** e-mail messages for each superhero.

TIPS

E-Mail Messages

- Include the name of the sender and the receiver in the heading. Also include a subject line to describe the contents of the e-mail.

  From: Rogue (sender)
  To: Superman (receiver)
  Subject: New Web site (subject line)

- Include a greeting (for example, Dear Rogue) and closing (for example, Yours truly, Superman).
- When writing real e-mails, always be polite.

D MEDIA *Creating Superheroes*

1. In the chart below, list **four** superheroes from comic books, games, movies, or TV shows. List some of their characteristics (for example, brave or honest) and special skills (for example, faster than a speeding bullet or able to fly).

Superheroes	Characteristics	Skills

2. Now create a Canadian superhero combining some of the skills and characteristics from your chart. Give your superhero a name and describe him or her.
3. Draw a picture of your superhero.

- Writers often use **comparisons** to improve their descriptions.

  EXAMPLE: Superman is <u>faster than</u> a speeding bullet.

  The above example compares Superman's speed to a bullet, and gives the reader the sense that Superman is fast. Comparisons can increase a reader's understanding of something, as well as adding colour to the writing.

- Comparisons that use the words **as**, **like**, or **than** are called **similes**.

  EXAMPLES: That lamp is <u>as</u> bright <u>as</u> the sun.
  Cari's new job is <u>like</u> a bad dream.
  Last summer was hotter <u>than</u> a volcano.

1. Choose a word from the word box to complete each simile.

bee	snake	rocket	judge	chicken

a. Rogue is as fast as a _____ .

b. The Green Hornet is busier than a _____ .

c. Superman acts like a _____, afraid to race Rogue.

d. The Riddler is sneakier than a _____ .

e. Batman is as honest as a _____ .

2. Create **five** similes for specific superheroes or super villains. Use **as**, **like**, or **than**.

a. _____

_____

b. _____

_____

c. _____

_____

d. _____

_____

e. _____

_____

Before Reading

What Canadian city would you like to travel to? _____

How would you like to get there? _____

Travel Challenge!

Article *by*
James Woodrow

Some TV shows ask ordinary people to race around the world and reach a final destination in order to win a prize. The people are given difficult tasks to complete along the way.

Taking part in such a race requires good communication skills and the ability to read maps, schedules, instructions, and other real-world texts. Winning the race means winning large cash prizes.

Could you win such a race? Take this Travel Challenge to find out!

TRAVEL CHALLENGE: Travel from Winnipeg to Saskatoon in less than ten hours without spending more than $150.

First Challenge: Examine this map, and then answer the questions on page 43. Use point form.

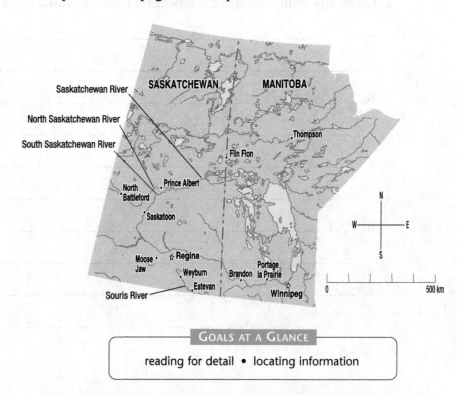

GOALS AT A GLANCE

reading for detail • locating information

1. What direction do you need to travel in to meet this challenge?

_____

2. Which provinces will you be travelling through?

_____

3. Use the scale of the map to calculate how far Saskatoon is from Winnipeg.

_____

Second Challenge: Read the bus schedule and answer the questions below. Note that the schedule is based on a 24-hour clock, which means that 16:50 is 4:50 in the afternoon, 23:50 is ten minutes to midnight, and so on.

WHITE WOLF BUS LINES
DAILY SCHEDULE – WINNIPEG/SASKATOON

Depart Winnipeg	Arrive Saskatoon	Depart Saskatoon	Arrive Winnipeg
09:30	18:00	07:45	16:20
10:00	18:00	09:00	17:20
16:50[1]	23:50	11:00	18:45
19:45 (Express)	01:45	19:30 (Express)	01:20
23:45	07:15	21:00[1]	05:45

[1]Friday only

FARES*

One-way: Adult $105   Student and Senior $85   Child under 12 $50
Return: Adult $185   Student and Senior $150   Child under 12 $80

* Taxes included

4. Put a star beside the bus you should take if you plan to leave Winnipeg on a Friday right after school.

5. Put a checkmark beside the shortest bus ride from Winnipeg to Saskatoon.

6. How much will it cost you to travel from Winnipeg to Saskatoon?

_____

Third Challenge: Read the airline ad and answer the following questions.

Canadian Getaway Airlines

Winnipeg to ...

Toronto	**$129**
Saskatoon	**$149**
Edmonton	**$189**
Vancouver	**$219**

Hourly departures!

During holiday periods, add $50.
Fares are one way. Return fares add $100.
Taxes not included.

7. Without reading the **fine print** [the small print at the bottom of the ad], how much does a one-way fare to Saskatoon cost?

_____

8. Read the fine print. How much does a one-way fare to Saskatoon actually cost if taxes are 14%?

_____

9. If the Travel Challenge took place during a holiday period, how much would airfare cost?

_____

Final Challenge: Combine all the information you have learned from these texts and answer the following questions.

10. Reread the **Travel Challenge**. To win the challenge, how must you travel to Saskatoon?

_____

11. How long will the trip take? _____

12. How much will the trip cost? _____

Use point form to answer these questions.

Use the map on page 42 to answer questions 1 to 4.

1. If you travel to Saskatoon by bus, will you spend more time travelling through Manitoba

   or Saskatchewan? _____

2. In which direction will you travel if you go to Moose Jaw from Saskatoon? _____

3. Name one city located between Winnipeg and Saskatoon. _____

4. Name one river located in Saskatchewan. _____

Use the bus schedule on page 43 to answer questions 5 and 6.

5. Why do you think there's an extra bus added to the schedule on Fridays? _____

   _____

6. The 09:30 bus from Winnipeg arrives in Saskatoon at the same time as the bus that leaves
   at 10:00. Why do you think they arrive at the same time?

   _____

Use the airline ad on page 44 to answer questions 7 and 8.

7. Which is cheaper? Circle **one**.
   a. a one-way trip by plane from Winnipeg to Vancouver in November?
   b. a one-way trip by plane from Winnipeg to Toronto during March break?

8. **a.** How much does it cost for a return trip from Winnipeg to Edmonton during February? _____

   b. How much does the same trip cost during the March break? _____

 9. Which do you find easiest to understand: maps, schedules, or ads? Why do you think
   the format you chose is easiest to understand?

   _____

   _____

 **Solving Math Word Problems**
- Focus on the important details in the problem. Circle or
  underline these details.
- Block out details that are unimportant.
- Make sure that you understand what the question is asking.
- Reword or rework the question using numbers.

1. The bus schedule on page 43 is a type of chart. Charts are a good way to organize information. Look at these sample charts.

Nutrition Information for Wheat 'n' Berries Cereal		
	175 mL of cereal	175 mL of cereal with 125 mL of 1% milk
Energy	145 Cal/480 kJ	205 Cal/730 kJ
Protein	4.8 g	8.9 g
Fat	1.7 g	2.1 g
Carbohydrate	34 g	50 g
Potassium	110 mg	300 mg

Prime Time TV Tonight							
	7:00	7:30	8:00	8:30	9:00	9:30	10:00
2	NewsHour	As Time Goes By	Red Green Show	Made in Canada	Basketball: Toronto Raptors at L.A. Lakers		
3	Star Trek		The X-Files		Movie: **** Pearl Harbor (2001)		
4	Labrador	The Rez	Buffalo Tracks		Movie: ** Jurassic Park III (2001)		

2. Develop **two** questions that can be answered by reading one of these charts. Ask a partner your questions. Answer his or her questions.

Question 1: _____

Answer 1: _____

Question 2: _____

Answer 2: _____

3. Explain how reading information in a chart can be easier than reading information in a paragraph.

_____

_____

_____

Charts
- Read the title of the chart and any information around the chart.
- Make sure you understand the type of information the chart is giving you.
- Read the headings for each column or row.
- Read one row or column at a time.

What major Canadian city would you like to visit? Use the Internet, newspapers, and/or travel brochures to plan a trip to that city.

1. Name of area you will be leaving from: _____

2. Name of city you will be travelling to: _____

3. Why would you like to go there? _____

   _____

4. Using a map, find the distance between where you live and the city you would like to visit.

   _____

5. Use the Internet or travel brochures to find **three** places to see in the city you are planning to visit. Use the chart below to record the information.

   Things to Do in _____

Event/Place	Admission Price	Hours

6. Find information about how to travel to the city you want to visit, and fill in the chart below. Show only the shortest times and the lowest prices in the chart.

Type of Transportation	How Long Does It Take to Get There?	How Much Does a Return Fare Cost?	What Days Can You Go?
Bus			
Plane			
Train			

7. Use the information above to write a one-page travel guide for the city you would like to visit. Include one paragraph for each event or place, and one paragraph for the best type of transportation. Include a photo or drawing of one of the city's tourist sites. Check your writing and correct any mistakes. Share this travel guide with a small group.

LANGUAGE CONVENTIONS *Proper Nouns*

> • A **proper noun** names a specific person, place, or thing, and begins with a capital letter.
>
> EXAMPLES: John, Teresa, Calgary, Western Transportation Line, Hamilton, January, Trans-Canada Trail, Aunt Pearl, Tuesday

1. Underline each proper noun in the sentences below. The first one has been done for you.

   a. Eric and Sean have been friends for years.

   b. His family will move from Winnipeg to Saskatoon in August.

   c. Uncle Dave lives in Regina.

   d. Max tells Sean to take an airplane.

   e. Plane fare from Winnipeg to Saskatoon costs $139 in November.

2. Write **four** sentences about where you live and the people you know. Circle the proper nouns you have used.

   a. _____

   b. _____

   c. _____

   d. _____

E MEDIA *Planning a Travel Challenge TV Show*

This selection states that there are some TV shows that ask people to compete in a race. These people (known as <u>contestants</u>) are often asked to complete challenging tasks as well. Think about what you would do to create a similar TV show.

1. How many people would race against one another? _____

2. How would contestants be eliminated from the race? _____

3. What cities or countries would contestants travel to? _____

4. What tasks or challenges would contestants need to complete along the way? _____

   _____

5. What resources (food, maps, money, vehicles, and so on) would the show provide? _____

   _____

6. What resources would the contestants need to provide for themselves? _____

   _____

7. What would the prize be? _____

Glance briefly at the poster. What part of the poster stays in your mind: the words or the picture?

I Should Still Have All My Fingers

Poster *from the Workplace Safety and Insurance Board*

VOCABULARY

punch press: a machine that cuts, stamps, or presses metal sheets using heavy blows

safety guards: barriers that protect a worker from injury

GOALS AT A GLANCE

identifying audience and purpose • analysing visual impact

A UNDERSTANDING THE SELECTION *Identifying Audience and Message*

Circle the <u>most</u> correct answer.

1. Megan's accident could have been prevented
   a. if the safety guards had been lower
   b. if her employer had provided a safe workplace
   c. if Megan knew she was also responsible for keeping her workplace safe
   d. all of the above

2. The main message of the poster is
   a. don't lose your fingertips
   b. it's your fault if you have an accident
   c. don't work in a filter factory
   d. you need to think about how safe your job is

3. The poster shows a young person because
   a. older workers don't have accidents
   b. young people look better in photos
   c. the poster's audience is young people
   d. most workplaces won't hire young people

B CRITICAL THINKING *Analysing Visual Impact*

1. What word best describes the look on Megan's face in the photo? _____ Explain your choice.

   _____

   _____

2. Imagine the poster without the photo. If it only had the words, do you think the poster would be as effective? Explain your answer.

   _____

   _____

3. a. **Circle** the words in the poster that are written in large type.

   b. Which of the words in large type make you want to read the poster? Why?

   _____

   _____

   c. Why do you think the poster is designed this way?

   _____

   _____

- A **slogan** is a short, easy-to-remember message.
- Advertisers often use slogans to sell products to their audience.

    EXAMPLES: The Workplace Safety and Insurance Board poster: <u>Safety starts with you</u>.
                      The United Way (a charity): <u>Without you, there would be no way</u>.
                      Nike: <u>Just do it</u>.

---

1. List **five** slogans you have seen in stores, on posters, or on TV. Include the product or service the slogan is advertising.

2. Choose the slogan you like best. Explain why you like it.

3. **a.** Write a different slogan for the poster on page 49.

Reflecting

    b. Explain why you think your slogan will appeal to your intended audience.

- A **singular noun** names one person, place, or thing.

  EXAMPLES: punch press, job, company

- A **plural noun** names more than one person, place, or thing.

  EXAMPLES: punch presses, jobs, companies, fingertips, filters

- Add **-s** to most nouns to make them plural.

  EXAMPLES: job – job<u>s</u>   fingertip – fingertip<u>s</u>

- Add **-es** to most nouns that end in **-ss**, **-x**, **-s**, **-ch**, or **-sh** to make them plural.

  EXAMPLES: press – press<u>es</u>   tax – tax<u>es</u>   bus – bus<u>es</u>
  church – church<u>es</u>   ash – ash<u>es</u>

- When a noun ends in a **consonant** + **-y**, change the **-y** to **-i** and add **-es**.

  EXAMPLE: company – compan<u>ies</u>

- When the noun ends in a **vowel** + **-y**, add an **-s** to make it plural.

  EXAMPLE: toy – toy<u>s</u>

Write the plural form of each noun below.

1. girl   _____

2. filter   _____

3. hand   _____

4. right   _____

5. press   _____

6. fax   _____

7. bay   _____

8. rash   _____

9. crash   _____

10. lady   _____

11. ax   _____

12. injury   _____

13. responsibility _____

14. guess   _____

15. fox   _____

UNIT 2 WRAP-UP

SELF-ASSESSMENT *Media Activities*

1. Check off each media activity in the list below that you completed during this unit:
   - ❑ creating a superhero chart
   - ❑ creating a Canadian superhero
   - ❑ creating a travel challenge TV show
   - ❑ identifying the audience and message of a poster
   - ❑ analysing the visual impact of a poster
   - ❑ creating a slogan

2. In your notebook, for one of the items you checked above, explain what you did and what you learned from completing the activity.

PROJECT IDEA *Superhero Poster*

In this unit you created a superhero (page 40) and a slogan (page 51). Combine what you learned in those activities to create a slogan and poster for your superhero. For example, Superman's slogan could be "faster than a speeding bullet."

Step 1. Describe your superhero. List at least **four** of his or her most important characteristics or skills.

_____

_____

_____

_____

Step 2. Choose one or more of the above characteristics or skills that your superhero will be known for. Create a short, catchy slogan based on the items you chose.

_____

_____

_____

Step 3. Test the effectiveness of your slogan by sharing it with a small group of classmates.

Step 4. Develop a poster that features your new slogan and an image of your superhero (see poster tips on page 86).

These tips can help you read and understand charts.

Title

The title tells you what the chart will be about. Ask Yourself: Does the chart hold information I need? What do I expect to find out by reading this chart?

Rows and columns

A chart is organized into rows and columns. The **rows** are horizontal, running from left to right. The **columns** are vertical, running from top to bottom. It's best to read a chart one row or column at a time. You might find it helpful to use your finger as you read along the row or column, especially in charts that use smaller type.

Headings

Ask Yourself: Do I understand how the chart is organized? What do the headings of each row or column tell me?

In this chart, the headings for each column tell what time a show is on, and the headings for each row tell which station a show is on. Note that, in this example, the words **Time** and **Channels** do not appear in the headings because it is assumed that people know this information.

Prime Time TV Tonight					
	7:00	7:30	8:00	8:30	9:0
2	News Hour	As Time Goes By	Red Green Show	Made in Canada	Basket at L.A.
3	Star Trek		The X-Files		Movie:
4	Labrador	The Rez	Buffalo Tracks		Movie:

Skimming

A good strategy to use with many charts is to skim for the information you want. For example, with this chart, you can skim for the show you want to watch and then figure out what time and channel it is on.

Checking

To check that you understand the information the chart is giving you, restate the information. For example, *The Rez* is on channel 4 at 7:30 (NOT on channel 7:30 at 4).

Setting Goals

What difficulties do you have reading and analysing charts? What can you do to improve this ability? Set **two** goals for analysing charts.

Before Reading
"Titanic Survivor: Eyewitness to Disaster"

A **KWL chart** (**K**now, **W**ant to Know, **L**earned) can help you recall what you already know about a topic and help you think about new ideas and information. Use a KWL chart to record information about the sinking of the ship *Titanic*.

K What I KNOW	W What I WANT to Know	L What I LEARNED

Using a KWL Chart

- In the first column of the chart, list what you already **KNOW** about the disaster of the ship *Titanic*.
- In the second column, list what you **WANT** to know about the ship or how and why it sank. List at least **three** questions.
- Look for answers to your questions as you read the following true account of one survivor, Ruth Becker.
- **After** you have read the true account, use the ideas and information you have **LEARNED** to write answers in the third column to your questions from the second column.

After Reading

Answer the following questions after reading the true account and completing the third column of the chart.

1. Did you find answers to all your questions? _____

2. If not, where else might you look for the answers? _____
_____

3. As you read the selection, did you think of any other questions? If so, list them below.
_____
_____
_____

Titanic Survivor: Eyewitness to Disaster

True Account *by Kate Shaftoe*

The *Titanic* set sail from Southampton, England, on Wednesday, April 10, 1912. Twelve-year-old Ruth Becker, her younger brother and sister, and their mother were among more than 2000 people to board the *Titanic*. It was the first voyage of the *Titanic*, and days earlier many experts had called it the safest ship in the world.

> **GOALS AT A GLANCE**
>
> visualizing the scene • organizing information

Ruth's mother was unsure about sailing on the *Titanic*. As soon as her family was on board she talked to a ship's officer about its safety. The officer reassured Mrs. Becker, saying the ship had watertight compartments that would keep the ship afloat if anything happened.

Four days later, the *Titanic* hit an iceberg and started to sink; its watertight compartments were flooded with water.

Mrs. Becker woke when the ship's engines stopped, and she heard running feet and shouting voices in the hallway. A passing steward told her to "put on your things and come at once."

Mrs. Becker rushed her children out of their cabins and up six flights of stairs to the top deck where the lifeboats were. It was about 12:30 in the morning on April 15, 1912.

The air on deck was icy cold. Other passengers wandered about, looking shocked and worried. There were only enough lifeboats for half the passengers. The Captain ordered women and children to board first. A sailor placed Ruth's brother and sister in one of the boats.

"This one's full," he announced.

"Please, you must let me go with my children!" cried Mrs. Becker. She was allowed to get in. But Ruth was still on deck.

"Ruth, quickly, get in another lifeboat!" her mother shouted.

Ruth calmly moved to the next boat and asked if she could board. The sailor lifted her into lifeboat number 13.

Finally, all the lifeboats were loaded and lowered. Ruth could see the people who remained on the sinking ship. They stood together for warmth. The decks of the *Titanic* were now slanted sharply. The **stern** [the rear of the ship] was lifted high out of the water. All the lights were still glowing, and the band continued to play.

Ask Yourself

If you were one of the passengers or crew aboard the *Titanic*, what would you be doing to survive?

What happened next was a scene of horror. The *Titanic* broke in half, and the **prow** [the pointed front part of the ship] slipped quietly into the water. For a few minutes, the stern section stayed upright. "And then…there fell on the ears the most terrible noise that human beings ever listened to, the cries of hundreds of people struggling in the icy cold water, crying for help with a cry that we knew could not be answered," Ruth recalls.

The horrible cries slowly died away. The people in the lifeboats knew the passengers and crew in the water were drowning or dying from the cold. A few lifeboats moved about, trying to help those in the water. But many of the lifeboats were overloaded and could take on no more survivors. Many of the people in the lifeboats fought to keep the people in the water away, afraid their lifeboats would sink. More than 1500 people died that night.

Ask Yourself
If you were one of the passengers in a lifeboat, would you help the people in the water? Why or why not?

Ruth and the other lifeboat survivors had to wait another two hours in the freezing night. Then they saw a light. Another ship, the *Carpathia*, had come to their rescue. Ruth was so numbed by the cold that she had to be pulled on deck. Ruth was reunited with her mother, brother, and sister the next day. They continued their journey to New York.

Ruth went on to become a schoolteacher and had three children. But her children did not know she had been on the *Titanic*.

Ruth did not speak about her experiences for almost 80 years. Before her death in 1990, she gave several interviews about the event. Even though so much time had passed, her memories were clear and detailed, as if it were only yesterday that the great ship had gone down.

DID YOU KNOW?

- Because of the *Titanic* sinking, the International Ice Patrol was created in 1913 to check for icebergs in the North Atlantic.

- A passing ship, the *Californian*, never answered the *Titanic's* call for help.

1. Write down at least **six** words to describe the scene Ruth witnessed the night the *Titanic* sank. Use words from the true account or words that came to mind as you read the selection.

_____ _____

_____ _____

_____ _____

2. Now, choose **one** of the following ways of representing the sinking of the *Titanic*.
   a. Draw the scene using pencils or paint, and add a caption.
   b. Write **one** paragraph to describe the scene. Include **three** facts from the true account.

EXTENDING: Share your work with a classmate, explaining what you've done.

B CRITICAL THINKING *Drawing Conclusions*

1. List **two** words to describe how you think Ruth felt when she set sail on the *Titanic*.

_____ _____

2. List **two** words to describe how you think Ruth felt when she was in the lifeboat.

_____ _____

3. List **two** words to describe how you think Ruth felt when she was rescued.

_____ _____

4. **a.** Why do you think Ruth did not tell her children about her experience on the *Titanic*?

_____

_____

   b. Why do you think Ruth later changed her mind about telling her story?

_____

_____

5. Why did so many passengers and crew members die when the *Titanic* sank?

_____

_____

EXTENDING: In a personal response journal, record your response to this selection. Consider these questions: Who do you think was to blame for this disaster? Why were women and children allowed in the lifeboats first? How do you feel about this?

C RESEARCHING *Organizing Information*

Think about a disaster that interests you (for example, Pompeii, the *Challenger*, or the explosion in Halifax Harbour). Research that disaster using these steps.

1. Create a **KWL chart** (**K**now, **W**ant to Know, **L**earned) to organize information on your chosen disaster.
2. Begin by filling in the first two columns. List at least **three** questions in the second column.
3. Research to find answers to your questions.
4. Use the information you discover to fill in the third column.

5. How useful do you find KWL charts for organizing information? Will you use KWL charts for other research projects? Why or why not?

_____

_____

_____

TIPS

Locating Information

- Visit the school library or public library. Ask a librarian to help you find the right section for your topic. She or he may even be able to recommend a good book.
- Use the library's computer or card catalogue to look for books and other sources.
- Use the Internet. (See the tips on page 70.)
- Ask experts (a history teacher, for example) about your topic.

D LANGUAGE CONVENTIONS *Possessive Form*

- The **apostrophe** (') and the letter **-s** are used to show that something belongs to someone. This is known as the **possessive form**.

   EXAMPLES: Ruth's mother
   The *Titanic's* lifeboats

1. Underline **one** example of an **apostrophe** used in this way in "*Titanic* Survivor: Eyewitness to Disaster."

2. Use an **apostrophe s** to change the following phrases to the possessive form.

   a. the life jacket belonging to Ruth _____

   b. the children of Mrs. Becker _____

   c. the stern of the ship _____

   d. the survival of the crew _____

   e. the cabin belonging to the Captain _____

1. "*Titanic* Survivor" uses many words related to ships. List **one** reading strategy you can use to figure out the meaning of these words.

_____

_____

2. All of the words in the crossword below are related to ships. Complete this crossword using the word that fits each clue in Across and Down.

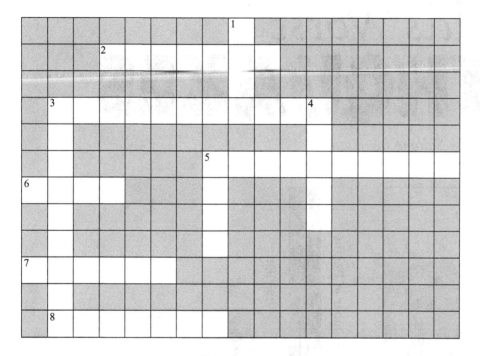

Across

2. famous ship that sank in 1912 (7 letters)

3. vests worn to prevent drowning (11 letters)

5. people travelling by ship (10 letters)

6. the floor of a ship (4 letters)

7. rooms on a ship (6 letters)

8. members of the ship's crew (7 letters)

Down

1. opposite of float (4 letters)

3. these are used to escape a sinking ship (9 letters)

4. the rear of a ship or boat (5 letters)

5. the front part of a ship or boat (4 letters)

EXTENDING: Chose **eight** different words from the selection and develop word puzzles (such as a crossword puzzle, word search, word jumble, or riddles). Ask a classmate to solve your word puzzles.

Before Reading

List **three** things you already know about earthquakes.

1.	2.	3.

The World's Worst
EARTHQUAKES

Visuals and Facts *created by Salome Benjamin*

A multi-storey building collapsed completely during the February 2002 earthquake in Sultandagi, Turkey.

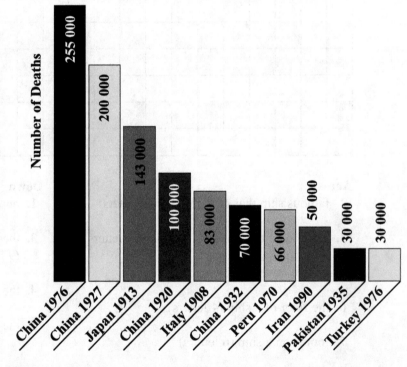

The World's Worst Earthquakes
This bar graph shows the number of deaths from the world's major earthquakes in the twentieth century.

GOALS AT A GLANCE

reading visual texts • synthesizing information

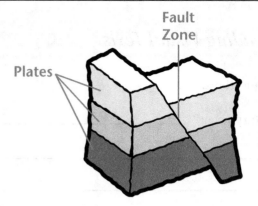

Fault Zone

Plates

What Causes Earthquakes?

Earthquakes happen when parts of the earth's crust shift. These shifting parts, called **plates**, are actually pieces of the earth's crust floating on the hot, molten interior of the earth. Most earthquakes occur along the edges of these plates and along weak areas of the crust called **fault zones**.

A powerful earthquake hit parts of western Japan in 1995, causing a section of the Hanshin Expressway to collapse.

Did You Know?

• The worst earthquake in history was in July of the year 1201 in the area of Egypt and Syria. The quake killed about 1.1 million people, the most deaths caused by any natural disaster in recorded history.

• At 9:00 p.m. on January 26th in the year 1700, a massive earthquake occurred along the west coast of Canada. This quake was one of the world's largest, probably measuring about 9 on the Richter scale. Experts know about this quake because it caused a **tsunami** (tidal wave) that swept across the Pacific Ocean and hit Japan, causing enormous damage. Also, the West Coast Aboriginal people have stories that tell of the damage caused by this quake.

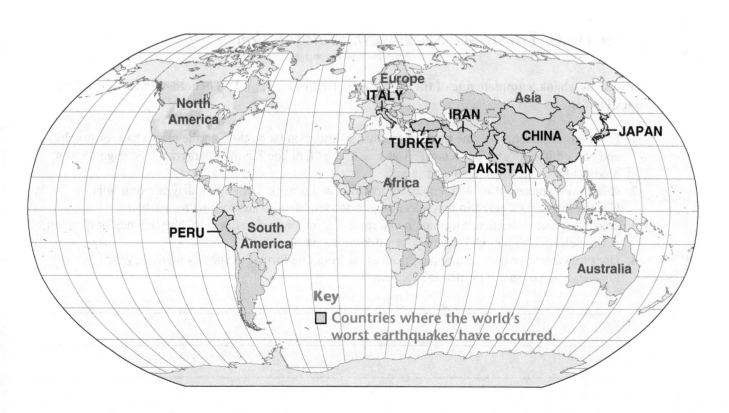

Key
☐ Countries where the world's worst earthquakes have occurred.

The World's Worst Earthquakes

Use point form or one or two words to answer these questions.

1. Where did the worst earthquake in the twentieth century occur? _____

2. What causes earthquakes? _____

   _____

3. How many people were killed in the year 1201 in Egypt and Syria? _____

4. How do you feel when you examine the photo on page 62? Explain your answer.

   _____

   _____

   _____

   _____

5. Which of the visuals (bar graph, map, photo, or diagram) did you find provided the most information? Explain your answer.

   _____

   _____

B   CRITICAL THINKING *Synthesizing Information*

In your notebook, complete <u>one</u> of the following activities (1, 2, <u>or</u> 3). Then answer the Reflecting question (4).

1. From this selection, take one piece of graphic information (something in the map, chart, or graph) and reword it as a "Did You Know?" Use one of the "Did You Know?" paragraphs on page 63 as a model. Share your work with a partner.

2. Take several pieces of related written information and rework them into a diagram or graph. Use the diagram or graph in this selection as a model. Share your work with a partner.

3. Take one piece of written information and rework it into a map or drawing. Use the map or the photo in this selection as a model. Share your work with a partner.

4. Does translating or transferring the information from one format to another increase your understanding of that information? Explain.

   _____

   _____

   _____

C VOCABULARY *Words About Earthquakes*

Reread "The World's Worst Earthquakes." <u>Underline</u> **all the words that have something to do with earthquakes. Use those words to solve the riddles below.**

1. The earth has one. So does a slice of bread. _____

2. When these shift they can cause earthquakes, unless they're in your kitchen cupboard. _____

3. Material beneath the earth's surface is so hot it's _____.

4. Earthquakes happen along weak areas of the earth's surface called _____ _____.

D MEDIA *Movie Poster*

Think about an image that might appear on a poster for a movie called *Earthquake*.

1. Describe the image. _____

_____

_____

2. List some words that might be added to the poster.

_____

_____

_____

3. Create a poster for this new movie. Your audience is teenagers who enjoy disaster movies, and your purpose is to persuade them to see the movie.

TIPS

Creating a Movie Poster

- Make sure your image grabs the audience's attention and creates interest about the movie.
- Choose the words for your poster with care. In as few words as possible, make your audience really want to see this new movie.
- Experiment with placing the words in different areas of the poster around or on the image.
- Remember to include the title: *Earthquake*.

Before Reading

Think about what you would do if you were caught in an earthquake.
As you read each tip below, think about why the authors are giving you this advice.

How to Survive an
EARTHQUAKE

How-to Article *from* The Worst-Case Scenario Survival Handbook
by Joshua Piven and David Borgenicht

VOCABULARY

debris: scattered fragments or rubbish

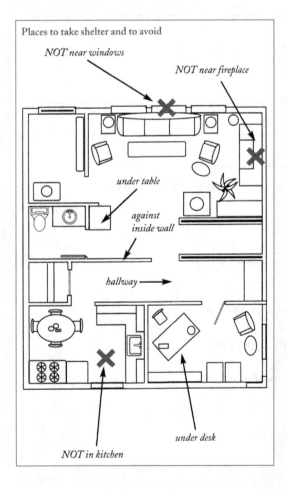

Places to take shelter and to avoid

NOT near windows

NOT near fireplace

under table

against inside wall

hallway →

under desk

NOT in kitchen

1. IF YOU ARE INDOORS, STAY THERE!

Get under a desk or table and hang on to it, or move into a doorway; the next best place is in a hallway or against an inside wall. Stay clear of windows, fireplaces, and heavy furniture or appliances. Get out of the kitchen, which is a dangerous place. Do not run downstairs or rush outside if the building is shaking. You could fall and hurt yourself or be hit by falling glass or debris.

2. IF YOU ARE OUTSIDE, GET INTO THE OPEN, AWAY FROM BUILDINGS, POWER LINES, CHIMNEYS, AND ANYTHING ELSE THAT MIGHT FALL ON YOU.

3. IF YOU ARE DRIVING, STOP, BUT CAREFULLY.

Move your car as far out of traffic as possible. Do not stop on or under a bridge or overpass or under trees, lampposts, power lines, or signs. Stay inside your car until the shaking stops. When you begin driving again, watch for breaks in the pavement, fallen rocks, and bumps in the road near bridges.

> **GOALS AT A GLANCE**
>
> making judgments • locating information

4. **IF YOU ARE IN A <u>MOUNTAINOUS</u> AREA, WATCH OUT FOR FALLING ROCKS, LANDSLIDES, TREES, AND OTHER DEBRIS THAT COULD BE LOOSENED BY QUAKES.**

VOCABULARY

mountainous: covered with mountains

5. **AFTER THE QUAKE STOPS, CHECK FOR INJURIES AND APPLY THE NECESSARY FIRST AID OR SEEK HELP.**

Do not attempt to move seriously injured people unless they are in further danger of injury. Cover them with blankets and seek medical help for serious injuries.

6. **IF YOU CAN, PUT ON A PAIR OF STURDY THICK-SOLED SHOES (IN CASE YOU STEP ON BROKEN GLASS, DEBRIS, ETC.).**

A powerful earthquake hit the Japanese port of Kobe in 1995. Over 200 people were killed and many were injured as trains were derailed and houses caught fire.

7. CHECK FOR HAZARDS.

- Fires
- Gas leaks
- Damaged electrical wiring
- Fallen or damaged utility lines
- Spilled medicines, drugs, or other harmful materials

8. CHECK FOOD AND WATER SUPPLIES.

Do not eat or drink anything from open containers near shattered glass. If the power is off, plan meals to use up frozen foods that will spoil quickly. Food in the freezer should be good for at least a couple of days. If the water is off, you can drink from water heaters, melted ice cubes, or canned vegetables. Avoid drinking water from swimming pools and spas.

9. BE PREPARED FOR AFTERSHOCKS.

Another, smaller quake may follow.

BE AWARE

- Use your telephone only for a medical or fire emergency; you could tie up the lines needed for emergency response. If the phone doesn't work, send someone for help.
- Do not expect firefighters, police, or paramedics to help you immediately. They may not be available.

In 1989, the top-deck section of a freeway collapsed onto its lower level when an earthquake hit the San Francisco Bay area.

A   **UNDERSTANDING THE SELECTION** *Reorganizing Information*

Use <u>your own words</u> to complete the following web. You can use point form.

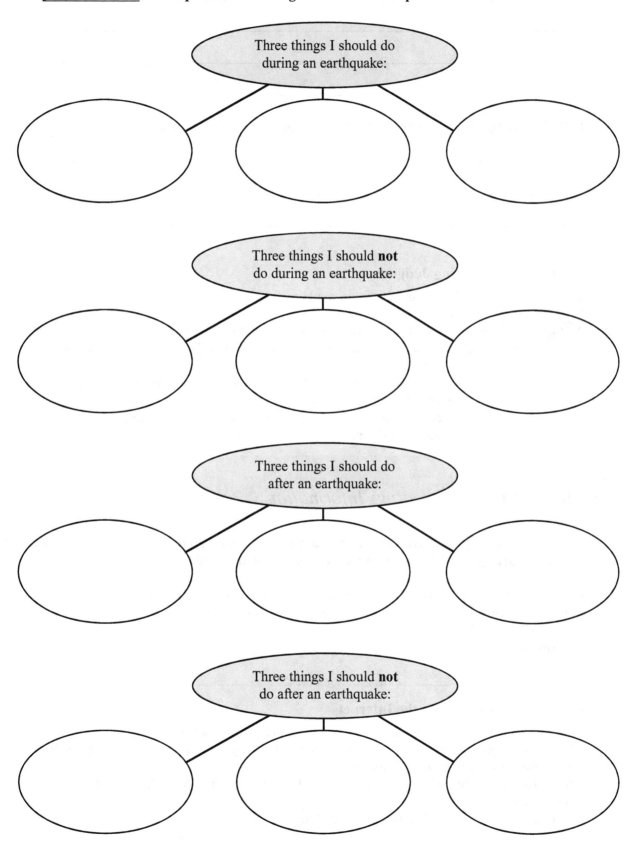

CRITICAL THINKING *Making Judgments*

1. Which **two** tips from the article are the **most** important? Explain your choices.

_____

_____

_____

2. Which **two** tips from the article are the **least** important? Explain your choices.

_____

_____

_____

Reading Strategies

Making Judgments

- Think about which tips would really save your life in an emergency. Those will be important tips.
- To choose the **two most** important tips, think about the tips that gave you ideas that you had never thought of before. You may find it helpful to rank the important tips.
- Think about which tips would **not** help save your life in an emergency. Those will be fairly unimportant tips.
- To choose the **two least** important tips, think about the unimportant tips that gave you information you already knew.

C

RESEARCHING *Locating Information*

Choose <u>one</u> aspect of earthquakes that you want to learn more about. What questions do you still have about earthquakes? Research to find answers to your questions.

1. Use the information you discover to write a one-page report on earthquakes.
2. Include at least one of the following: a chart, graph, map, photo, or diagram.
3. Include one "Did You Know?"
4. Share your report with the class.

> **TIPS**
>
> ### Locating Information on the Internet
>
> - Choose a suitable search engine, such as Google, AltaVista, or Yahoo.
> - Use an appropriate search word or phrase. For example, if you want to find out about earthquakes in Canada, use **Canadian earthquakes**.
> - Scan the titles in the list of sites that appears. Click on those sites that seem to be the most useful for answering your questions.
> - Most search engines will list the most likely sites first.

D VISUAL COMMUNICATION *Creating a Floor Plan*

Examine the simple <u>floor plan</u> (the diagram of an apartment) on page 66.

1. Use a **red** pen to circle areas to avoid during an earthquake. Use a **blue** pen to circle areas that are safe during an earthquake.
2. Now, create a floor plan of your home. Use the floor plan on page 66 as a model. Remember to include furniture, doors, windows, and stairs.
3. On your floor plan, use a **red** pen to mark areas to avoid during an earthquake. Use a **blue** pen to mark the safe areas.

EXTENDING: On your floor plan, mark a good escape route in case of fire. First, decide and mark where in the house the fire has started, and then decide how best to get out of the house, avoiding the fire and smoke.

E LANGUAGE CONVENTIONS *Adjectives*

- An **adjective** is a word that describes a noun or a pronoun. Adjectives can describe **what kind**, **which one**, or **how many**.

    EXAMPLES: <u>massive</u> earthquake
    <u>inside</u> wall
    <u>heavy</u> furniture

- Colourful adjectives can help the reader to see a scene or character more easily.

1. <u>Underline</u> **five** adjectives in the selection. In the margin beside each word you underline, explain what that adjective does. Does it describe what kind, which one, or how many?

2. From the box at right, choose a good adjective to complete each sentence.

    nine
    injured
    best
    dangerous
    inside

    a. The _____ place to be in an earthquake is under a desk.

    b. Stand against an _____ not an outside wall.

    c. The kitchen is a very _____ place to be.

    d. Do not move seriously _____ people.

    e. There are _____ steps to follow in this selection.

3. List at least **three** colourful adjectives to describe each type of disaster below.

    a. earthquake _____ _____ _____

    b. flood _____ _____ _____

    c. forest fire _____ _____ _____

    d. volcano _____ _____ _____

    e. explosion _____ _____ _____

Before Reading

Whenever you read a newspaper article, the following strategies are good to keep in mind.

Newspaper Articles

- Read the **headline** (the title of the article). What does it tell you about the subject of the article?
- Examine any photos and read their **captions** (the text beneath the photo). What do they tell you about the subject of the article?
- As you read, look for answers to the 5 Ws and H: Who? What? Where? When? Why? How?

Mock Disaster
Tests Region's Resources

Newspaper Article *by Leslie Ferenc*
Thursday, May 30, 2002, from The Toronto Star

VOCABULARY

mock: an imitation, not real

simulation: an invented model or event that mimics a real one

It was like a scene right out of the latest disaster movie. Dozens of bleeding passengers were hurried out of a train that had hit a gas tanker truck on Timothy Street in Newmarket (north of Toronto in Ontario).

It's as close as Peggy Martin and friend Barbara Bell want to be to the real thing. These two seniors were among 50 volunteers who took part in a mock disaster yesterday. The simulation was called Exercise Timothy, and was the first test of York Region's emergency plans. These simulations help to prepare emergency workers for real disasters, such as a plane crash or a tornado.

For a moment, it all seemed too real.

Martin said there was confusion on the train. "People were screaming and crying."

"People were calling out for their mothers, others were trying to get to the next train to find relatives and friends. The actors did a good job," said Bell.

> **GOALS AT A GLANCE**
> evaluating sources • writing headlines

Both Martin and Bell agreed that the experience was an eye-opener about what to do and not to do in an emergency.

Outside the train, fire crews hosed down the tanker truck. The truck had been placed on its side on the Timothy St. railway tracks. York Region police roped off the accident scene and moved people out of a seniors' building. Ambulance workers moved the injured to safety.

"Things are going well and all the systems are working," said York Region Police Inspector Eugene Kerrigan. "The system seems to have served its purpose and we're ready if something should happen."

"There's room for improvement," Duty Inspector Dennis LaPlante said. Throughout the three-hour exercise, he was looking for weak links. He found several mistakes. For one, cars sitting in the Timothy St. parking lot made it difficult to shift the large <u>triage</u> buses. That wasted time getting the injured to hospital.

The cars, he said, should have been moved out of the way. "I think we need to have another exercise," LaPlante said. "Practice makes perfect."

The exercise took a year to plan and involved more than 200 people. It included regional staff, hydro workers, doctors, nurses, and volunteer victims.

Newmarket Mayor Tom Taylor said the mock disaster helped put his mind at ease. "After the process, I feel safer in terms of our ability and the region's ability to respond if something happens in the future."

VOCABULARY

triage: the sorting of a number of victims from worst to least injured so that those with the greatest need can be treated first

Did You Know?
In Egypt, in February 2002, more than 373 people died in a train fire. A small cooking stove being used by a passenger caused the fire. The train continued moving, in flames, for kilometres, before the driver became aware of the fire. Each of the flaming railway cars held more than twice the passengers it was designed for.

Training Day: Emergency Services staff work with volunteer casualties (as well as crash test dummies, shown here) during the disaster drill. More than 50 people agreed to act as wounded victims during the simulation.

1. Complete the following chart. If you can only answer **three** of these questions, you need to reread the article.

Who was involved?
What has happened?
Where did it happen?
When did it happen?
Why did it happen?
How did people feel about the outcome?

2. In a small group, discuss your answers. Are all your answers the same as your classmates' answers? List a few reasons why answers might differ.

_____

_____

_____

> • Reporters include **quotations** in their news reports to show that they have used **reliable** sources.
> • Reporters also use quotations to present **both** sides of an issue.
> • They may quote **witnesses**. They may also quote **experts** who can explain why something happened, or why it is important.

1. **a.** Underline **one** quotation in the article that helps the reader understand what it was like to take part in the simulation.
   b. Circle the speaker's name. In the margin, label the speaker **witness** or **expert**.
   c. Is this speaker a reliable source? Explain why or why not.

   _____

   _____

   _____

2. **a.** Underline the **two** quotations in the article that give different opinions about the success of the simulation.
   b. Circle each speaker's name. In the margin, label each speaker **witness** or **expert**.
   c. Are both speakers reliable sources? Explain why or why not.

   _____

   _____

   _____

   _____

   d. Explain why these people have different opinions about the success of the simulation.

   _____

   _____

   _____

3. List the names of **two** other people quoted in the article. Explain why you think their opinions are important.

   _____

   _____

   _____

WRITING *Headlines*

1. Think of **two** other headlines that could have been used for this article. Write them below.

_____

_____

2. Which headline do you think is best? Discuss your choice with a classmate.

> **TIPS**
>
> **Headlines**
> - Headlines should be short and easy to read.
> - Headlines should clearly summarize what an article is about.
> - Headlines should grab a reader's interest.

D LANGUAGE CONVENTIONS *Verbs*

> - A **verb** is a word that expresses an action or state of being.
>   EXAMPLES: do, see, think, scream, be, seem, find, agree, say

1. Underline the verbs in the sentences below.
   a. It was like a scene out of a disaster movie.
   b. The train hit a gas tank.
   c. Many volunteers took part in the mock disaster.
   d. These simulations help people prepare for real disasters.
   e. There is room for improvement.

> - **Vivid verbs** are strong, descriptive verbs. They give the reader a better understanding of what is happening. Using vivid verbs in your writing can increase its power.

2. Check the sentence below that you think sounds most powerful.
   a. My brother shouted out his answer from across the park, and then he ran for home.
   b. My brother bellowed out his answer from across the park, and then he bolted for home.

3. Replace each underlined verb below with a more vivid verb. You may want to use a thesaurus.

   a. The passengers called for help. _____

   b. The train hit a car. _____

   c. The truck flew through the air. _____

   d. The tornado blew the cow into the next town. _____

   e. The townspeople ran up the hill, away from the flooding river. _____

Before Reading
"The Bridge Came Tumblin' Down"

"The Bridge Came Tumblin' Down" is a song about the collapse of the Second Narrows Bridge in Vancouver in 1958.

1. Look at the map. What two areas does the bridge join?

   _____

2. Imagine you're one of the people in this photo. Write one sentence to describe what you are thinking.

   _____

   _____

   _____

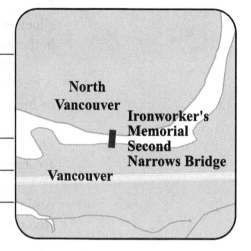

Did You Know?
The Ironworker's Memorial Second Narrows Bridge was completed and opened in August of 1960. Altogether, 25 workers died during the building of this bridge. Plaques are placed at both ends of the bridge in memory of these workers.

The Bridge Came Tumblin' Down

Song *by Stompin' Tom Connors*

Nineteen <u>scarlet</u> roses the <u>chaplain</u> spread around,
In the waters of Burrard Inlet, in old Vancouver Town, where the bridge
    came tumblin' down.
When the bridge came tumblin' down, nineteen men were drowned,
In June of nineteen fifty-eight, in old Vancouver Town.

There were seventy-nine men working to build this brand new bridge,
To <u>span</u> the Second <u>Narrows</u> and connect up with the ridge, till a big wind
    hit the bridge.
And the bridge came tumblin' down, and nineteen men were drowned,
And the medical <u>corps</u> couldn't be too sure of the rest of the men they found.

In among the twisted <u>girders</u>, one man realized,
How last night, he'd been dreaming and saw before his eyes the big wind
    on the rise.
And the bridge came tumblin' down and nineteen steel men drowned,
And he saw the fright of the darkest night, in old Vancouver Town.

With <u>frogmen</u> in the water, by cutting torches' glow,
They fought to save the steel men from certain death below and pain we'll
    never know.
When the bridge came tumblin' down and nineteen men were drowned,
And sixty more that came ashore, so thankful they were found.

It often makes you wonder, in strength, who has the <u>edge</u>,
The longest <u>steel-beam structure</u>, that spans the highest ridge, or the men that
    built the bridge.
For the bridge came tumblin' down, and nineteen men were drowned,
But the other men came back again, to lay the new beams down.

Now, if you're ever crossing this mighty bridge <u>sublime</u>,
And nineteen scarlet roses pass before your mind, remember and be kind.
The bridge came tumblin' down, and nineteen men were drowned,
So you could ride to the other side of old Vancouver Town.

A UNDERSTANDING THE SELECTION *Responding Personally*

Use complete sentences to answer the following questions.

1. What part of this song did you like best? Explain why.

_____

_____

_____

2. **a.** How does the last line in the song make you feel?

_____

_____

   b. Explain why you think this is (or is not) a good way to end the song.

_____

_____

3. Why do you think people write songs about disasters?

_____

_____

B CRITICAL THINKING *Analysing Characteristics*

1. Read over the following checklist, which lists the characteristics of a **ballad**. Check off each characteristic of a ballad that you think applies to the song "The Bridge Came Tumblin' Down."

   Ballad Checklist
   ❏ Ballads usually tell a story.
   ❏ Ballads are often about love, disasters, or outlaws.
   ❏ The lines in a ballad often rhyme.
   ❏ Ballads often include **dialogue** (words in quotation marks that tell what someone said).
   ❏ Ballads often contain lines that repeat, with some variations, after each verse.

2. Do you think "The Bridge Came Tumblin' Down" is a typical ballad? Why or why not?

_____

_____

_____

C LANGUAGE CONVENTIONS *Joining Sentences*

- Use **conjunctions** to join short sentences.

  EXAMPLE: The bridge fell. Soon workers came to rebuild it.
  The bridge fell, <u>but</u> soon workers came to rebuild it.

- Here are some common conjunctions to use when joining sentences.

  because   or   when   for   where
  and   if   since   unless but

- Joining sentences can add variety to your writing.

Join the short sentences using one of the conjunctions from the list above. Check that your new sentence makes sense. The first one has been done for you.

1. Nineteen men died. The bridge collapsed.

   <u>Nineteen men died when the bridge collapsed.</u>

2. The bridge fell. There were strong winds that day.

   _____

3. Sixty men were rescued. Nothing could save the others.

   _____

4. Think about those workers. You cross the bridge.

   _____

5. Don't call an ambulance. There is a real emergency.

   _____

D WRITING *Newspaper Article*

Choose <u>one</u> of the following headlines and then write a 100-word newspaper article about the collapse of the Second Narrows Bridge.

- 19 Workers Dead!
- Bridge Collapses, Killing Workers
- 60 Workers Survive, 19 Die, When Bridge Collapses

1. Use "Mock Disaster Tests Region's Resources" as a model for your article.
2. Use information from the song, photo, and map to help you answer the **5 Ws and H**. (Who? When? Where? What? Why? How?).
3. Try to use some words from the song.
4. Remember to use conjunctions to join sentences.

SELF-ASSESSMENT *Using Graphic Organizers*

1. Choose **one** item below. In your notebook, describe the strategies you used to help you read or use the graphic organizers.

   ❏ using KWL charts for reading and researching
   ❏ organizing information in webs
   ❏ using a checklist to analyse characteristics
   ❏ creating a floor plan
   ❏ reading bar graphs, maps, scales, or diagrams
   ❏ using bar graphs, maps, scales, or diagrams within your writing

2. Reflect on the graphic organizers in this unit. Based on your experiences, create a list of **five** tips for reading or using graphic organizers.

PROJECT IDEA *Front Page News*

Work with a small group to create the front page of a newspaper after a disaster.

Step 1. As a group, think about all the selections you read in the *Disasters* unit. Choose **one** disaster or type of disaster that interests your group the most. Now, each group member needs to independently write an article about the disaster, such as an eyewitness account, a science article, or an article on its future impact.

Step 2. In your notebook, create a KWL chart (see page 55) for that disaster. Research the disaster to answer the questions in the second column of your KWL chart. Fill in the third column of the chart.

Step 3. Use your KWL chart and information from your research to write your newspaper article.

Step 4. Use at least **five** of the words below in your article. Only use a word if you know its meaning or are willing to check a dictionary.

natural disaster	massive	emergency	ignite	victims
damage	earthquake	horror	triage	flames
courage	tremors	debris	tornado	collapse
rescuer	sinking	aftershock	casualties	sublime
survivor	lifeboat	paramedic	fire	corps

Step 5. Write a headline for your article. Check that your article answers the 5 Ws and H (see page 72).

Step 6. Include at least **one** photo or illustration and at least **one** diagram, graph, or map.

Step 7. With your group, arrange all the articles to look like the front page of a newspaper. Give your newspaper a name.

Before starting to research Pompeii, a student created the following KWL chart. In the <u>first</u> column, she listed what she already knew. In the <u>second</u> column, she listed some questions she had about Pompeii. After doing the research, this student completed her KWL chart by filling in the <u>third</u> column with answers to the questions she asked in the second column. She also made a correction in the first column because she found out something new during her research.

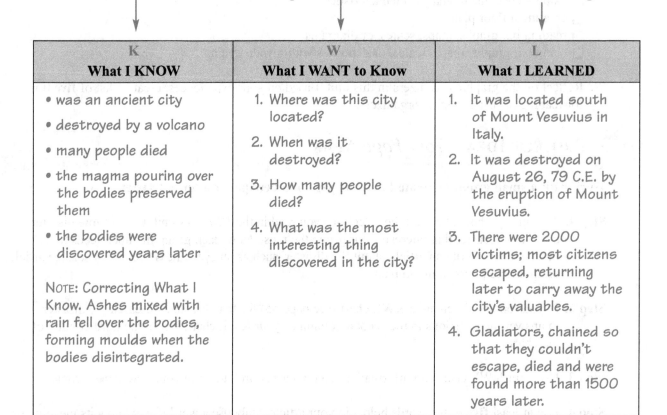

Before Researching		After Researching
K **What I KNOW**	**W** **What I WANT to Know**	**L** **What I LEARNED**
• was an ancient city • destroyed by a volcano • many people died • the magma pouring over the bodies preserved them • the bodies were discovered years later NOTE: Correcting What I Know. Ashes mixed with rain fell over the bodies, forming moulds when the bodies disintegrated.	1. Where was this city located? 2. When was it destroyed? 3. How many people died? 4. What was the most interesting thing discovered in the city?	1. It was located south of Mount Vesuvius in Italy. 2. It was destroyed on August 26, 79 C.E. by the eruption of Mount Vesuvius. 3. There were 2000 victims; most citizens escaped, returning later to carry away the city's valuables. 4. Gladiators, chained so that they couldn't escape, died and were found more than 1500 years later.

After completing the chart, this student wrote the following paragraph about the disaster of Pompeii:

Pompeii was an ancient Italian city destroyed on August 26, 79 C.E. by the massive eruption of the volcano Mount Vesuvius. While many people fled the city, 2000 people died and were buried by ash. Some of the victims were gladiators who could not escape because they were chained up. Ash and rain falling over the victims formed moulds that would be discovered by archaeologists more than 1500 years later, even though the bodies themselves had disintegrated. These moulds helped tell the story of Pompeii and its victims.

Before Viewing

A poster uses words and images to send a message to an audience. Often, posters try to persuade or convince an audience to do or buy something. Think of a poster that you believe worked really well (for example, one for a movie or concert). List **three** things that you think made that poster effective:

_____

_____

_____

Poster Expressions

Posters *from Various Sources*

Six out of these twelve women will die from smoking.

Which number are you?

List **three** things you notice in this poster.

_____

_____

_____

Emily King, a student, won first prize in a contest with this poster design that uses photos of her friends. The contest was run by *In 2 Print* magazine and Health Canada.

List **three** things you notice in this poster.

_____

_____

_____

This poster is one in a series produced by the United Way to promote its services and encourage community support. This series features the life stories of many different people in many different situations.

Dream Big Dreams.
Small Dreams Have No Magic.

My name is Junior Kayi. I was born in the Congo. I lived there until the civil war broke out and people came to my house. I hid myself under my bed. All I heard was the crying of my parents and my Dad saying: "Don't hurt her." When the cries were over, there were bodies on the floor. A family member helped me escape and put me on a plane. I just slept and slept. When I woke up, I was in Canada. I felt I was in heaven. What kept me going was United Way and something my Dad always told me: "Dream big dreams because small dreams have no magic."

At United Way, I met some great people who believed in me. I learned computer and business skills and how to speak English. When the classes were finished, I used to stay till they kicked me out. That's how hard I worked. Today, I run my own e-business company. If you ever wonder what happens to the money that you give to United Way, remember me. Thank you for giving. Your money got to me.

WITHOUT YOU, THERE WOULD BE NO WAY
1-800-267-8221

 **United Way**

Reading Strategies

Posters
- Think about the poster's **design** (the use of colour, the placement of images and words, and the text type: the shape and weight of letters).
- Identify the poster's **message** (what it is trying to say).
- Identify the poster's **audience** (who it is for: teenagers, adults, and so on) and its **purpose** (why it was created: to persuade someone to do or buy something, and so on).

A UNDERSTANDING THE SELECTION *Responding to a Poster*

Choose one of the posters. Answer all of the following questions for that poster.

1. What is the poster's message? Write the poster's message in your own words.

_____

_____

2. **a.** How does the poster make you feel?

_____

_____

    b. Why do you feel this way?

_____

_____

    c. Do you think the poster's creator intended you to feel this way? Explain.

_____

_____

3. Return to the list of three things you liked or noticed about the poster. Explain why you chose those three things.

_____

_____

4. Think about how you would change either the words or the image(s) to make the poster more effective. Mark up the poster, showing at least **three** ideas.

B CRITICAL THINKING *Analysing Audience and Purpose*

With three classmates, choose one of the posters to discuss. Use the following questions as a starting point. Choose one group member to make point-form notes.

- What is the purpose of the poster?
- Did the poster succeed in its purpose? Why or why not?
- Who do you think was the original audience for the poster? (Clues to audience are included in the poster and in the information at the bottom of each page.) Why do you think so?
- What do you think about the poster's design?
- What other questions or ideas do you have about the poster?

EXTENDING: Meet with a group that discussed the other poster. Share your answers.

MEDIA *Creating a Poster*

1. Choose an issue that you feel strongly about. Use the following worksheet to develop ideas for a poster to communicate your feelings on the issue. Your **purpose** is to convince an **audience** of your peers that your point of view is correct.

Issue: _____

Note your stand on the issue (for or against). _____

List **three** ideas for your poster. Keep in mind your purpose and audience.

_____

_____

_____

_____

List ideas for the poster's design and production (colours, size, use of type, use of computer technology).

_____

_____

_____

2. Develop a rough draft of your poster on a small sheet of paper.
3. Create a final draft of your poster on a large sheet of paper.
4. Put up your poster in your classroom.

EXTENDING: Write a paragraph to explain how your poster communicates your feelings about the issue, and what you hope the reaction of viewers will be.

TIPS

Posters

- Use one or more strong images. You might create drawings, use photos, or find good images on the Internet or in magazines.
- Arrange the words and images effectively, so that the viewer's eye is drawn immediately to a strong image.
- Choose colour and text type to capture the viewer's attention.
- Develop a short, clear **slogan** (a short, easy-to-remember message) that communicates your point of view on the issue.

Before Reading

Do you play video games? If **yes**, what do you like about video games? If **no**, why not? How do other people you know feel about video games?

_____

_____

_____

VIDEO GAME WORLD

Essay *by Oswin Chang*

It's an exciting time to be a teenager. We've made incredible <u>progress</u> in technology over the past few <u>generations</u>. It's almost hard to imagine life without portable CD players, DVD players, cell phones, or home computers. Some of the most amazing developments in the past few years are in the world of video games.

Some people are quick to criticize video games, but I think they're overlooking the positive <u>aspects</u>. Fantasy and science fiction games are two of my favourite types of games, because they take you to a whole new world, in a much more physical way than books and stories. It's easy to spend a whole afternoon caught up in a good game! Then there are <u>strategy games</u> that fire up the mind, and action games that really get your blood pumping. Video games have proven themselves as a quality form of entertainment.

The video games of today are a lot more sophisticated than the video games that your parents used to play. Every day, they get even more realistic, and fun, and even <u>addictive</u> (in a harmless way). And through the Internet, we can now play against people in other cities, and even countries. What a great way to make new friends!

Who knows what the games of tomorrow will bring. Maybe we will be able to play in more realistic, <u>three-dimensional</u> environments. Maybe we will see new kinds of game controllers, that might use the whole hand, or even the whole body, so that we don't have to suffer from Nintendo-thumb any more. Hopefully, we will see a broader range of fun and exciting new kinds of games. But one thing is for certain: video games are here to stay!

VOCABULARY

progress: an advance or improvement

generation: all people born around the same time: your parents belong to one generation; you and your friends belong to another generation

aspect: a way of looking at something or a way of viewing a subject

strategy games: games that require critical thinking and planning

addictive: something that creates a habit that is difficult to control

three-dimensional: having, or appearing to have, depth, height, and width

> **GOALS AT A GLANCE**
>
> comparing viewpoints • writing opinions

Complete this summary of "Video Game World."

Oswin Chang believes that it's an _____ time to be a teenager, because

of the incredible _____ in technology, especially in the world of

_____.

Chang points out that some people _____ video games.

He thinks they are overlooking the positive _____. He enjoys playing fantasy

and science fiction games because they open up a whole new _____.

He thinks video games are a quality form of _____.

Chang explains that video games today are more _____. He thinks games

are _____ in a harmless way. Chang says that through the Internet we can

play against people in other _____ and countries, and make new

_____.

Chang suggests that in the future, video games will be more _____.

We may play in _____ environments,

using the whole hand or _____. Chang feels video games are here to

_____.

B **VOCABULARY** *Word Riddles*

Use the words from the vocabulary list on page 87 to solve each riddle.

1. I am just one side of a subject and there may be many other sides. What am I? _____

2. Positive advances in technology are due to me. What am I? _____

3. If you can't stop playing a game, call it _____ .

4. I have height, width, and depth. I am _____ .

5. There are many types of video games, but this type requires critical thinking. _____

_____

6. You belong to one. Your parents belong to another. What are these? _____

C CRITICAL THINKING *Comparing Viewpoints*

Reread the essay "Video Game World." Read and look at the comic strip below. Answer the following questions using complete sentences.

1. Why do you think the father in the comic strip wants Jeremy to "do something else for a while"?

_____

_____

2. What might Jeremy say to defend his playing video games all day?

_____

_____

3. What do you think Oswin Chang, the author of "Video Game World," would say in response to this comic strip?

_____

_____

D WRITING *Opinions*

1. I like/dislike (**circle one**) video games, because _____

_____

2. Some people pester me about playing video games, because they think _____

_____

3. I agree/disagree (**circle one**) with these people, because _____

_____

EXTENDING: Use the ideas above to write a paragraph that explains your opinion of video games.

- Use a **period** (.) to end a statement or command. A **statement** tells you something. A **command** orders or requests you to do something.

  EXAMPLES: **statements**: My name is Junior Kayi. I was in Canada.
  commands: Stop smoking. Give money to the United Way.

- Use a **question mark** (?) to end a question. A **question** asks you something.

  EXAMPLES: Which number are you?   Who is Junior Kayi?
  What happened to Junior?

1. Add the correct punctuation to the end of each sentence in the following paragraph.

    When you read a poster, you should ask yourself several questions___ Who is the audience___ What is the purpose of the poster___ What is the poster's message___ Answer these questions, and you will have a better idea of what the poster is trying to do and why it was produced___ Also, remember to look at the poster's design___ Think about how the image(s) and words work together___ How does the poster make you feel___ Discussing the poster with others is always helpful___ How do other people feel when they look at the poster___ If they feel differently, why do they___ Comparing your responses to the poster with others can give you new ideas___

- Use an **exclamation mark** (!) to end an exclamation. An **exclamation** is a sentence that expresses strong feelings.

  EXAMPLES: Video games are here to stay! What a great way to meet people!
  Watch out!

2. End each sentence below with the correct punctuation mark: an exclamation mark, a question mark, or a period.

   a. Who's going to play video games with me___
   b. I enjoy playing video games___
   c. I love video games___
   d. What a night___
   e. Did you go to Nancy's party___
   f. Who else went___
   g. I had a great time___
   h. What a terrific baseball game___
   i. Who was playing___
   j. Careful___

TIPS

Punctuation Marks

- Do not overuse exclamation marks in your writing. Save this punctuation mark for when you really want to express strong feelings.
- When you're reading, punctuation marks can help you figure out where to pause, where to stop, and where to put emphasis.

Before Reading

Rock-and-roll music has been a part of our culture for over 50 years. Rock-and-roll was born in the United States in the 1950s, a combination of rhythm and blues and country music. Young people of the fifties welcomed rock-and-roll, a style of music they could call their own. Here's a brief history of the music that changed the world.

Rock-and-Roll: The First 50 Years

Timeline *by Judy Jupiter*

The Fifties

1951   Disc jockeys at radio station KOWH in Omaha introduce a "Top 40" show that plays all the hits all the time. Their show is inspired by watching people play the same juke box song over and over again.

1953   The Crows release "Gee," which some consider to be the first rock-and-roll song. Elvis Presley makes his first record.

1954   Disc jockey Alan Freed uses the term **rock-and-roll** for the first time on radio.

1955   Bill Haley and the Comets release "Rock Around the Clock."

1957   Chuck Berry releases the hits "School Day" and "Rock And Roll Music."

1959   Buddy Holly, the Big Bopper, and Richie Valens are killed in a plane crash: known as "the day the music died."

> **GOALS AT A GLANCE**
>
> analysing cause and effect
> conducting personal interviews

Jimi Hendrix.

The Sixties

1962   Chubby Checker's song "The Twist" becomes the new dance craze.

1964   The Beatles land in America, leading the British music invasion.

1965   "Back in My Arms" by The Supremes rises to the top of *Billboard's* singles chart. The group sets a record: most **consecutive** (one after another) Number One hits by an American group.

1966   The Beach Boys' album *Pet Sounds* has everybody "Surfin' USA."

1969   The Woodstock Music and Arts Festival brings thousands of music fans to Max Yasgur's farm in New York. Performers include Joan Baez, Jimi Hendrix, Janis Joplin, and The Who.

The Seventies

1970   The Beatles break up. Janis Joplin dies of a drug overdose.

1973   Pink Floyd releases *Dark Side of the Moon*.

1975   The Patti Smith Group releases *Horses*. Patti Smith will later have a huge impact on Punk music.

1977   Elvis Presley dies.

1979   The Who releases two movies and goes on a world tour.

Fans at a 1970s concert. How has music changed since then?

The Eighties

1980 John Lennon is murdered outside his New York apartment building.

1981 Tina Turner begins her comeback as a solo artist and opens for The Rolling Stones.

1982 Michael Jackson releases his album *Thriller*.

1984 Bruce Springsteen, the "Boss," releases *Born in the USA*.

1986 The Rolling Stones receive a Lifetime Achievement Grammy Award.

1987 Billy Joel tours and records an album in Russia.

The Nineties

1991 The Barenaked Ladies release an independent cassette that hits the Top 20 and goes platinum, a first for an independent release in Canadian history.

1992 Seattle becomes the home of Grunge Rock with groups such as Nirvana and Pearl Jam.

1993 Irish supergroup U2 completes its two-year Zooropa world tour.

1995 The Rock and Roll Hall of Fame and Museum opens in Cleveland. Alanis Morissette releases *Jagged Little Pill*, her first album, which goes on to have four hits.

1997 Sarah McLachlan organizes Lilith Fair, a tour that showcases women singers and songwriters. It's the most successful tour of 1997 and continues in 1998 and 1999.

A UNDERSTANDING THE SELECTION *Recalling Details*

Choose the correct answer from the box to complete each statement.

1. _____ made his first record in 1953.

2. _____ led the British Music Invasion.

3. _____ had the most consecutive Number One hits by an American group.

4. _____ was one of the performers at Woodstock.

5. _____ toured Russia in 1987.

| The Supremes |
| The Beatles |
| Billy Joel |
| Janis Joplin |
| Elvis Presley |

B CRITICAL THINKING *Analysing Cause and Effect*

1. With a small group, discuss how rock-and-roll affected the people who listened to it. Think about how rock-and-roll changed the way people danced, dressed, and talked. In your notebook, record **three** ideas from your discussion.
2. With your group, discuss how you have been affected by music (for example, rock-and-roll, rap, hip-hop, or jazz). In your notebook, record **three** ideas from your discussion.

EXTENDING: For question 2, develop a cause-and-effect chart to show the effect a particular type of music has had on you (see model below).

Cause-and-Effect Relationships

- To analyse cause-and-effect relationships, first identify the cause (for example, sleeping in).
- Then identify the effect or effects caused by that initial event (for example, getting to school late, getting a detention).
- You can use arrows to represent cause-and-effect relationships, as in the cause-and-effect chart following:

sleeping in ⟶ getting to school late ⟶ getting a detention

- Using a chart to show cause-and-effect relationships can help you identify earlier causes too (in the above example, it might be: getting to bed late).

C RESEARCHING *Conducting Personal Interviews*

Choose <u>one</u> time period from this selection that interests you.

1. Investigate the music of that time period further. Use the Internet, print sources, and personal interviews.
2. Create a timeline to present your information. Use "Rock-and-Roll: The First 50 Years" as a model.
3. You should have at least **five** new entries that are not already part of this selection.

> **TIPS**
>
> **Personal Interviews**
>
> • List **five** questions about your topic. Include questions that require more than a yes/no answer.
> • List **five** experts on the topic you can ask for an interview (for example, family and friends interested in music or a local disc jockey).
> • Ask your questions clearly and politely.
> • Choose the information that will be most useful for your purpose.

D LANGUAGE CONVENTIONS *Present Tense*

> • The **tense** of a verb tells the time of the action, feeling, or state of being. The **present tense** tells what is happening now or tells about an ongoing action.
>
> > EXAMPLES: James <u>sings</u> as he <u>enters</u> the house. (happening now)
> > I <u>like</u> rock-and-roll music. (an ongoing action)
>
> • The present tense is often used in timelines and captions. Check that you have used the present tense in your timeline in activity C.
>
> > EXAMPLES: Elvis <u>releases</u> his first album.
> > Janis Joplin <u>performs</u> at Woodstock.
>
> • When you're reading a selection, pay attention to the verb tense that the author is using. Think about what the verb tense tells you about the action.

Use the present tense of the verb in parentheses to complete each sentence below.

1. Jason _____ (break) his latest record.

2. The school _____ (announce) a new program.

3. You _____ (love) rap music.

4. I _____ (know) it will be a long concert.

5. We _____ (want) to be on time.

Before Reading

Ethan Moses is a New York high school student and photographer. His school is very close to the site of the World Trade Center towers. He was there on September 11, 2001 when two planes piloted by terrorists struck the towers. What do you remember about how you felt the day of that tragedy?

_____

_____

_____

Make Sure No One Ever Forgets

Photo Essay *by Ethan Moses*

GOALS AT A GLANCE

evaluating purpose and message
analysing the photo essay

I felt guilty for days after running from the dust cloud of the second World Trade Center tower collapsing, guilty that on top of being so lucky as to escape with my life, I had the nerve to shoot pictures of the **demise** [death] of thousands. I spoke with my father's friend from Bronx Science who is now a photographer for ConEd. Both of us, like many others who photographed the collapse of the WTC, did so with tears in our eyes. I told him that I was ashamed to be taking pictures, but he said that it was our responsibility. He told me that through our photographs, even more than our writing, the world would remember what happened on September 11, 2001.

I told my father that I would **venture** [go] out with my camera to take pictures. I felt sorry that I had moped around the house and wandered Lower Manhattan for the last four days, without taking any pictures. I felt guilty that I had let the sorrow of my fellow New Yorkers, as well as my family, go unrecorded. I felt a responsibility to take pictures because I was there, I ran from the debris cloud, and even more horribly, thought my father, mother, and many family friends were inside or in **adjacent** [nearby] buildings. I told my father that for the sake of my children, and my children's children, he should do the same and go help to record history.

He said that he had been in bed crying for the past two days. He couldn't watch the news, and couldn't look at the pictures. I've always known he wasn't able to look at pictures of the Holocaust or of the Vietnam War without wincing and turning away. This is because when he saw the pictures of Vietnam and World War II, they conveyed to him at least a little of the **trauma** [suffering] that those who were there lived through. The reason we should be taking pictures is so that 30 or 60 years from now, people will see them and have to turn away.

To all of you, if you can bring yourself to do it, please take some pictures that will capture the present suffering, and unity in America. Write about it. Make sure no one ever forgets.

1. a. Explain Ethan Moses' purpose in creating this photo essay. What is his message?

_____

_____

_____

b. Do you agree with his message? Why or why not?

_____

_____

_____

2. a. Why does Moses take photos of the disaster?

_____

_____

_____

b. At first, how does Moses feel about the photos he has taken?

_____

_____

c. How does Moses feel by the end of the selection?

_____

_____

3. How does Moses' father feel about photos that show the victims of war or tragedy?

_____

_____

4. Do you think the title "Make Sure No One Ever Forgets" is a good title for this photo essay? Why or why not? If not, what would you call the photo essay?

_____

_____

_____

B CRITICAL THINKING *Analysing the Photo Essay*

1. Examine each of the photos in "Make Sure No One Ever Forgets."
   a. What caught your attention first?

   _____

   _____

   _____

   b. Which photo do you find most effective in showing the events or experiences of people on September 11, 2001? Why?

   _____

   _____

   _____

   c. Analyse the photographic effects (for example, the background and foreground, the use of shadow or lines) in the photo you chose for question 1b.

   _____

   _____

   _____

2. Describe how you felt after reading "Make Sure No One Ever Forgets."

   _____

   _____

   _____

EXTENDING: Use one of the following formats to record your response to Moses' photos: a poem, song, response journal, diary entry, story, collage, drawing, or another format of your choice. Develop your response to these photos and then share it with a partner.

C MEDIA *Creating a Photo Essay*

Follow these steps to create a photo essay.

1. Use "Make Sure No One Ever Forgets" as a model.
2. Choose a topic for your photo essay: war, school sports, friends, and so on.
3. Find at least **three** strong photos to represent your topic, or take three good photos.
4. Write a paragraph to explain the purpose of your photo essay.
5. Arrange your photos and paragraph in a pleasing way.

D VOCABULARY *Synonyms*

Find the following words in "Make Sure No One Ever Forgets": <u>demise</u>, <u>venture</u>, <u>adjacent</u>, <u>trauma</u>. Notice how each of these words has been defined by placing a <u>synonym</u> (a similar but easier word) in brackets beside the first word.

1. List **four** other words from the photo essay that a reader might find difficult.

   a. _____   b. _____

   c. _____   d. _____

2. For each word you have listed, write down a synonym that could be used in its place. If necessary, use a dictionary or thesaurus to help you.

   a. _____

   b. _____

   c. _____

   d. _____

NOTE: When you see words in square brackets (**[ ]**) in an original selection, it usually indicates that those words have been included by someone other than the author. In this case, the editor included synonyms that would be easier to understand.

E LANGUAGE CONVENTIONS *Past Tense*

- The **past tense** is used to tell about something that happened in the past. The action is over.

   EXAMPLES: His friend <u>worked</u> for ConEd.   I <u>moped</u> around the house.
   I <u>felt</u> guilty for days.   He <u>said</u> that he had been in bed.

- The past tense is usually formed by adding **-ed** to the end of the verb. Words ending in **-e** just need a **-d** added.

- However, there are many irregular verb forms in the past tense (for example, <u>felt</u> for **feel**, <u>said</u> for **say**, and <u>was/were</u> for **be**).

Complete each sentence below by using the past tense of the verb in parentheses.

1. I _____ (venture) out with my camera.

2. The disaster _____ (happen) more than five years ago.

3. We _____ (talk) about taking photos of the people and the city.

4. Everyone _____ (survive) the fire last night.

5. We _____ (photograph) the scene with tears in our eyes.

SELF-ASSESSMENT *Media*

1. Choose **one** item below. In your notebook, explain what you learned about this media activity or skill.
   - ❏ analysing the audience and purpose of a poster
   - ❏ creating a poster
   - ❏ analysing the message in a comic strip
   - ❏ developing your opinion on a media issue
   - ❏ evaluating the purpose and message of a photo essay
   - ❏ analysing a photo essay
   - ❏ creating a photo essay

2. Think back to all of the media selections in this unit. In your notebook, describe the selection you most enjoyed reading or viewing. Explain why you enjoyed it. Describe the selection that you think you handled with the most success. Explain what helped you succeed.

PROJECT IDEA *Opinion Piece*

Follow these steps to develop an opinion piece on a media issue.

Step 1. Choose one of the following statements to write about. You can either write in favour of the statement or offer an opposing viewpoint. Beside the statement you choose, record your position on the issue. (I agree/I disagree)

   - ❏ TV shows are too violent. _____

   - ❏ Video games are not a waste of time. _____

   - ❏ Rock-and-roll (or other types of music) is too commercial. _____

   - ❏ Cigarette companies should be allowed to advertise on TV. _____

   - ❏ Photographers and journalists should report on tragedies and disasters. _____

   - ❏ Your own choice of issue: _____

Step 2. Conduct personal interviews to find out how others feel about the issue. Think about their viewpoints and the support they give for their opinions.

Step 3. Write one paragraph explaining what the issue is, how you feel about it, and why you feel that way.

Step 4. Write a second paragraph to include support for your position.

Step 5. Write a third paragraph explaining any opposing viewpoints. Try to include an explanation of why you don't agree with these viewpoints.

PARAGRAPH 1
The Issue
PARAGRAPH 2
Support
PARAGRAPH 3
Opposing Views

EXTENDING: If someone in your class has written an opinion piece on the same topic but with a different opinion, together, present your opinions to the class.

Read the following paragraph. Note how causes and effects have each been labelled.

CAUSE

CAUSE

EFFECT

EFFECT

In the past several years, reality TV shows have become very popular, both with the networks and the TV audiences. These shows **are cheaper to produce** than many shows that use expensive actors, so many networks quickly began to see how important it was to add them to the prime-time lineup. **Audiences were bored with the regular lineup**, stale sitcoms and dramas, so reality shows attracted large audiences. The audiences wanted something new and original. Of course, now, there are a ton of reality shows on TV; shows that really just copy other shows. Audiences are becoming bored with these shows, too.

EFFECT

Now, take a look at the chart below. This cause-and-effect chart shows the relationship described in the paragraph. It's more complicated than the cause-and-effect chart on page 94, because the relationships are more complicated.

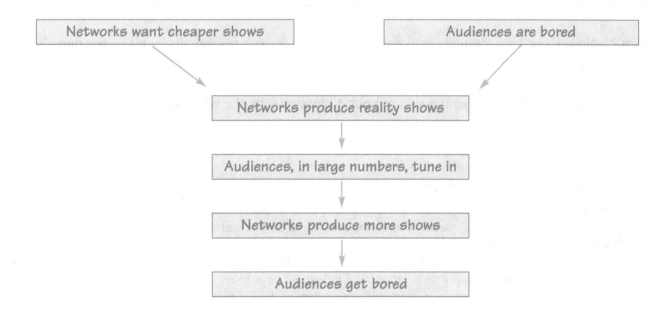

Before Reading
"The Choice"

Step 1. **Think** about the following questions for several minutes:
- If you could know the future, would you want to?
- Why or why not?
- What are the **pros** (advantages) and **cons** (disadvantages) of knowing the future?

Record your thoughts on the following chart.

Would You Want to Know the Future? (Check one.)	
Yes _____ No _____ Maybe _____	
Because...	
Pros of Knowing the Future	**Cons of Knowing the Future**

Step 2. Now, share your thoughts with a **partner**. Listen as your partner shares his or her thoughts. Did anything your partner say make you change your mind?

Step 3. Together, **share** the main points of your discussion with the whole class.

Think, Pair, Share

The "think, pair, share" strategy can be used whenever you're asked a question, or are responding to stories and non-fiction.
- First, **think** about the question on your own.
- Then, **pair** up with a partner and talk about your ideas.
- Finally, **share** your ideas, and your partner's, with a small group or with the whole class.
- Using this strategy can help you work out your own ideas about a subject.

During Reading

Read this story about a person who visits the future using a time machine. Think about the choice the time traveller makes.

The Choice

Science Fiction Story *by W. Hilton-Young*

Before we sent Sue Williams into the future, she bought a notebook, camera, and video camera. That night, when all was ready, she and I made coffee. Sue might want some coffee, if she came back.

"Goodbye," I said. "Don't stay too long."

"I won't," Sue answered, checking the settings on the time machine one last time. "Goodbye, Jack."

I watched her carefully.

Sue hardly seemed to move at all. She was back from her time trip a second after she had left. It seemed that way, at least, by our sense of time.

We had not been sure how long Sue would be away. Maybe a minute. Maybe several years. But here she was, as if she had never left.

"Well?" I asked.

"Well," she said, "let's have some coffee."

I poured it out, waiting for her to say something. As I gave her a cup, I said again, "Well?"

"Well, the thing is, I can't remember," she said with a confused look.

"Can't remember? Not a thing?" I pushed her for some answer.

> **GOALS AT A GLANCE**
>
> retelling the story • representing the scene

Sue thought for a moment and then said sadly, "Not a thing."

"But your notes? The camera? The video camera?" I insisted.

The notebook was empty, and the indicator of the camera was set at "1" still. The tape was not even loaded into the video camera.

"But why?" I asked. "How did it happen? Can't you remember anything?"

Again, she thought for a minute and then nodded. "I remember only one thing," she answered.

"What?" I asked, impatiently.

"I was shown everything. Then I was given the choice of whether I should remember it or not, after I got back," Sue spoke slowly.

"And you chose not to? But what an odd thing to…" I declared.

"Isn't it?" Sue interrupted. "I can't help wondering why."

A UNDERSTANDING THE SELECTION *Retelling the Story*

1. Discuss this story with a partner. Use questions such as the following:
   - What do the characters (Jack and Sue) want at the beginning of the story?
   - What happens to the characters?
   - How does the story end?
2. Now, retell the story to your partner in your own words. To **retell** a story means to tell the story to someone in a new way. Tell what happened.

B CRITICAL THINKING *Forming Questions*

1. What questions do you think Jack and Sue have **before** Sue travels to the future? List at least **two** questions.

   _____

   _____

   _____

2. What questions do you think Jack and Sue have **after** Sue returns from the future? List at least **two** questions.

   _____

   _____

   _____

3. What do you think the future that Sue sees will be like?

   _____

   _____

   _____

C VISUAL COMMUNICATION *Representing the Scene*

Imagine that Sue has created a drawing to show what the future looks like.

1. List at least **five** things that might be in her drawing.

   _____

   _____

2. Create a drawing to show what Sue sees in the future.
3. Check that your drawing reflects the future suggested in the story.

D WRITING *A Paragraph*

1. Think about these questions from page 104:
   • If you could know the future, would you want to?
   • Why or why not?
   • What are the pros and cons of knowing the future?
2. Write a paragraph about knowing the future.

Reflecting

3. Think about the answers you gave to the questions both before and after reading the story. Did your answers change? If so, how and why?

E LANGUAGE CONVENTIONS *Quotation Marks*

- **Quotation marks (" ")** are used to show that someone is speaking. This story uses a lot of quotation marks because there is a lot of **dialogue** (spoken words) between the characters.

  EXAMPLE: "I remember one thing," she answered.

- Place **end punctuation** (periods, question marks, and exclamation marks) for a spoken sentence before the last set of quotation marks.

  EXAMPLES: "I can't remember anything."
  "Can you remember anything?"   "I remember nothing!"

- If the sentence in quotations should end in a period, but is followed by a **speech tag** (for example, he said, she asked), use a comma instead. When a sentence ends with a question mark or exclamation mark, a comma is not used.

  EXAMPLES: "I was shown everything," Sue said.
  "What were you shown?" I asked.   "Everything!" she cried.

- Use a comma after the speech tag when it comes before the quotation and use a capital letter for the first word in the quotation.

  EXAMPLES: She said sadly, "Not a thing."   I asked, "How did it happen?"

Add the correct punctuation to the following examples of dialogue.

1. "What time is it___" he asked.

2. She replied___ "It's almost six___"

3. "We're late___" she shouted.

4. I asked___ "How long will you be gone___"

5. She said___ "About five hours___"

6. I yelled___ "I can't wait that long___"

EXTENDING: Reread the last two lines of "The Choice." In your notebook, write **four** more lines of dialogue that could be added to this story. Make sure you use speech tags to show who is speaking. Punctuate your dialogue correctly.

Before Reading

Can you solve this puzzle?

What is **it** that we can't live without? Our bodies are made up of 66% of **it**. Seventy percent of the earth's surface is covered with **it**. Without **it** plants and animals could not exist. Can you guess what **it** is?

It is *water*, one of our most valuable natural resources.

Water Just the Facts!

Statistics *from CBC News Online by Owen Wood*

◊ More than **24 million** Canadians use **municipal** [city or town] drinking water in their homes.

◊ There are about **4000** municipal water-treatment plants in Canada. These water-treatment plants clean the water taken from lakes, rivers, and **ground water** [underground] sources, and they make the water fit to drink. But less than **3%** of municipally treated water is used for drinking.

◊ The average adult drinks **1.5 L** (that's less than a large pop bottle) of water daily, including water used in drinks such as coffee, tea, and juice.

◊ In 1998, the average Canadian used about **300 L** of water **daily** inside the home (enough to fill an average bathtub about three times). That's **twice** as much water as the average European uses.

◊ Most indoor water is used in the bathroom.

◊ People watering their lawns and gardens use **50%** of all treated water.

◊ Dripping taps and other leaks cause **20%** of all municipal drinking water to be wasted.

A Breakdown of Water Used in Canadian Homes

This is a pie graph developed using information from Environment Canada. Information is based on the average amount of water used in Canadian homes.

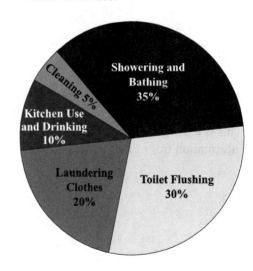

GOALS AT A GLANCE

analysing information • interpreting graphs

Average Amount Drunk Per Canadian in 2000

This is a pictograph developed using information from Statistics Canada. Information is based on sales of beverages.

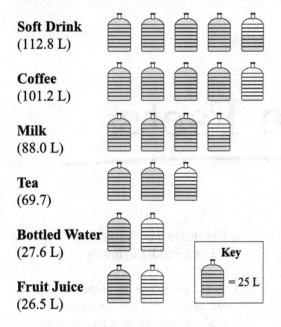

Soft Drink (112.8 L)

Coffee (101.2 L)

Milk (88.0 L)

Tea (69.7)

Bottled Water (27.6 L)

Fruit Juice (26.5 L)

Key = 25 L

- **One hundred percent** of Canadians living in towns and cities can get clean water. This figure is **99%** for Canadians living in **rural areas** [the country]. Compare this to Afghanistan, where only **11%** (in the country) and **19%** (in the cities and towns) of people can get clean water.

- Around the world, about **34 000** people die each **day** due to diseases related to water or dirt. In developing countries, **80%** of illnesses are water-related.

- In May 2000, **7** people died in Walkerton, Ontario when E. coli and other bacteria contaminated the town's water supply. Over **2000** people got sick.

- In 1993, **100** people died in Milwaukee, Wisconsin, because of an outbreak of the water-borne parasite Cryptosporidium. About **400 000** people got sick.

- Canada has about **20%** to **25%** of the world's fresh water.

- More than **1 trillion litres** of untreated sewage (waste from toilets and other drains) are dumped into Canadian waters every year by **21** cities across the country.

Amount of Water Used Per Task

This is a bar graph developed using information from Environment Canada.

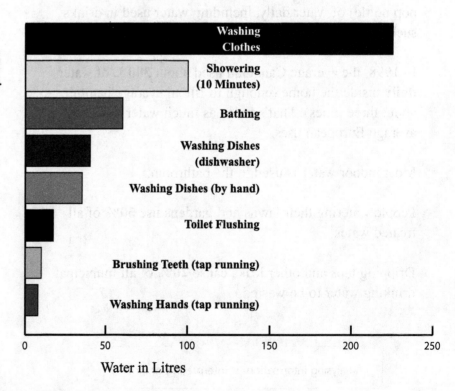

Washing Clothes

Showering (10 Minutes)

Bathing

Washing Dishes (dishwasher)

Washing Dishes (by hand)

Toilet Flushing

Brushing Teeth (tap running)

Washing Hands (tap running)

0   50   100   150   200   250

Water in Litres

A UNDERSTANDING THE SELECTION *Recalling Facts*

1. Write **true** or **false** after each statement below.

   a. More than 24 million Canadians use municipal drinking water. _____

   b. Less than 3% of municipally treated water is used for drinking. _____

   c. The average adult drinks 15 L of water daily. _____

   d. Most indoor water is used in the kitchen. _____

   e. Watering lawns and gardens uses 90% of all treated water. _____

2. Reread or skim the selection so that you can correct each of the above facts that you marked **false**. Circle the part of the statement that is wrong. Then write the correct fact above the original statement.

B CRITICAL THINKING *Analysing Information*

1. With a small group, discuss the significance or importance of at least **five** of the water facts. For example, why is it significant that so little treated water is used for drinking? Assign one group member to take point-form notes.

2. Now, have each group member take on one of the following roles and discuss the same facts again. For example, an environmentalist might comment that using drinking water on lawns and gardens is a waste of energy and water.
   • an environmentalist
   • a scientist who studies water sources and treatment
   • a worker in a water treatment plant
   • someone who lives in a city where the sewage is untreated
   • a plumber
   • someone from a country with very little fresh, clean water

   Each group member should make at least **one** statement about at least **one** fact. Support your statements with personal knowledge and ideas about the subject.

3. With your group, discuss how changing your perspective changed your reaction to some of the facts.

C   READING *Interpreting Graphs*

Look at each graph on pages 109 and 110.

1. Circle **one** fact that surprised you. Explain why you were surprised. _____

_____

2. <u>Underline</u> **one** fact that you found interesting. Explain why. _____

_____

3. For **each** graph, take **one** fact and make it a statement. For example, the second last row of the pictograph could be stated like this: On average, Canadians drank 27.6 L of bottled water in 2000.

   Pictograph: _____

   _____

   Pie graph: _____

   _____

   Bar graph: _____

   _____

EXTENDING: Choose an appropriate type of graph (pictograph, pie graph, or bar graph) to present the following information: In the year 2000, every Canadian ate, on average, 142 kg of fresh vegetables, 11 kg of canned vegetables, and 6 kg of frozen vegetables. Create the graph that best illustrates this information. Share your graph with a partner.

D   ORAL COMMUNICATION *Presenting Facts*

1. Highlight **one** fact from "Water: Just the Facts!" that you think everyone should know. In your notebook, write how you feel about that fact, and why you think it's important.
2. Practise reading the fact, and what you have written about it, out loud.
3. Present this information to your class.

> **TIPS**
>
> **Presenting Effectively**
> - Speak clearly and slowly.
> - Speak with appropriate expression and emphasis.
> - Stand up straight.
> - Make eye contact with audience members.
> - Look to the left, right, and centre, often.

- A **comma (,)** shows a pause in thought in a sentence, but it is not a full stop.
- Use a comma between words or groups of words in a series.

  EXAMPLE: Treatment plants clean water from lakes, rivers, and ground water sources.

---

1. Go back to "Water: Just the Facts!" and circle **one** example of a comma used in the above way.

2. Add commas where needed in the following sentences. The number of commas each sentence needs is indicated in brackets.

   a. Water is used in drinks such as coffee tea and juice. (2)

   b. People water flowers lawns and vegetable gardens. (2)

   c. Drinking water is wasted by watering lawns cleaning and flushing toilets. (2)

   d. Canada's lakes ponds streams and rivers cover thousands of square kilometres. (3)

   e. Canada supplies fresh water to the United States Mexico Greenland and Brazil. (3)

- Use a comma before a **conjunction** (<u>and,</u> <u>but,</u> <u>or</u>) in a compound sentence.

  EXAMPLE: Great Bear Lake is the largest lake that lies entirely within Canada, <u>and</u> it is more than five times the size of Prince Edward Island.

---

3. Go back to "Water: Just the Facts!" and <u>underline</u> **one** example of a comma used in the above way.

4. Add commas where needed in the following sentences. Each sentence needs one comma.

   a. Great Bear Lake is large but it is not as large as the Pacific Ocean.

   b. Niagara Falls is the largest producer of electric power in the world and it is a major tourist attraction.

   c. Almost all Canadians can get clean water but only some people in developing countries can.

   d. Showers and baths use 35% of water in the home and laundry uses 20%.

   e. People can drink tea or they can drink coffee.

TIPS

Using Commas
- When you're writing, if you're not sure you need a comma, say the sentence aloud. Add a comma whenever you hear a slight pause in the flow of the writing. A full stop would need a period or other end punctuation mark.
- Think about how a comma changes the meaning of the sentence you are reading or writing. Does the sentence make more sense with or without the comma?

Most of the world uses fossil fuels (such as coal, oil, and natural gas) to create energy. But these fuels create pollution and are also running out. So countries around the world are looking for new ways to create and save energy. The following selection shows what some countries are doing.

Energy-Saving Ideas for a New World

Facts and Map *adapted from Yes Mag*

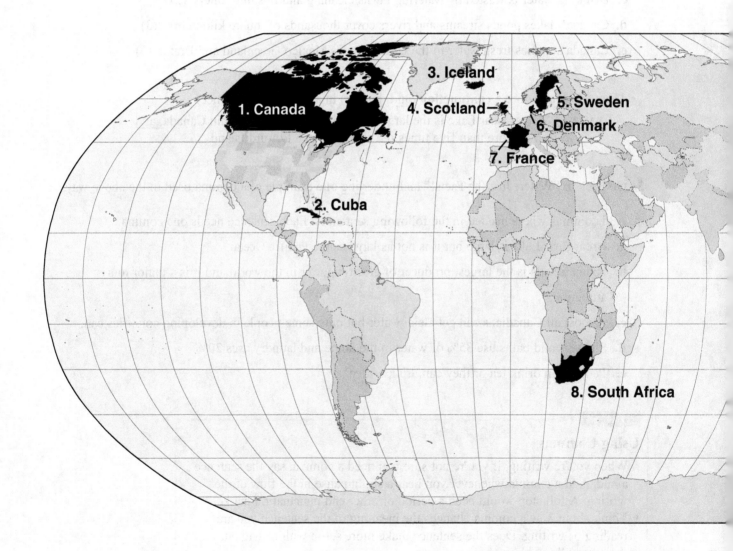

1. Canada
2. Cuba
3. Iceland
4. Scotland
5. Sweden
6. Denmark
7. France
8. South Africa

GOALS AT A GLANCE

making connections • developing research questions

1. **THE SUN SHINES ON CANADA**

   The power of the sun is beaming down on Canada's waterways. Of Canada's nearly **20 000** lighthouses, beacons, and buoys, **5000** use solar power to guide boats on their way.

2. **CUBA'S SWEET IDEA**

   Cuba grows sugar cane and exports it to countries around the world. It also burns sugar to supply almost **30%** of the country's energy.

3. **ICELAND FREEZES OUT FOSSIL FUELS**

   Iceland plans to stop using fossil fuels by the year 2020; it is turning to cleaner, more efficient hydrogen as a fuel source.

4. **SCOTLAND HARVESTS WAVES**

   On the Island of Islay, the energy created by sea waves is used to power about **400** Scottish homes.

5. **SWEDEN GOES FOR GRAINS**

   In Sweden, people are filling up small cars and trucks with canola oil rather than gas. This alternative fuel is also available in other countries.

6. **DENMARK WINS WITH WIND**

   Denmark uses the energy of the wind to produce almost **10%** of its electricity. By the year 2030, the country hopes that **50%** of its energy will come from wind turbines (an engine driven by wind).

7. **FRANCE TURNS THE TIDE**

   A region of France called Brittany is using ocean tides for **90%** of its power needs. China, Canada, and Russia also have tidal power plants.

8. **SOUTH AFRICA TURNS ON THE SUN**

   Switching from a heavy use of coal, South Africa is exploring the use of more solar power. Beginning in November 1998, one multimillion-dollar project hoped to supply **50 000** rural homes with electricity produced using solar power.

9. **JAPAN DOES THE WAVE**

   Japan has an **$8 million** floating experiment called the "Mighty Whale." This power plant uses sea waves to produce enough electricity to power about **15** homes.

UNDERSTANDING THE SELECTION *Recalling Details*

Circle the correct response to finish each statement. Once you have answered all the questions, return to the selection and check your answers.

1. To generate power, Japan's "Mighty Whale" power plant uses the energy of the
   a. tides   **b.** sun   **c.** sea waves   **d.** wind

2. Scotland uses wave power to provide power to
   a. 4 homes   **b.** 400 homes   **c.** 4000 homes   **d.** 40 homes

3. By the year 2030, Denmark hopes to increase its electricity production from wind turbines to
   a. 50%   **b.** 60%   **c.** 90%   **d.** 10%

4. By the year 2020, Iceland will be using hydrogen as a fuel source because it is
   a. cheaper and easier to get than other fuels
   b. cleaner and more efficient than other fuels
   c. more powerful and cheaper than other fuels
   d. none of the above

5. Sweden's small cars and trucks can fill up on
   a. sunflower oil   **b.** olive oil   **c.** hazelnut oil   **d.** canola oil

6. Canada uses solar power to fuel
   a. lighthouses   **b.** beacons   **c.** buoys   **d.** all of the above

7. According to the article, the following countries all have tidal power stations
   a. Brazil, Russia, Japan, South Africa
   b. France, Denmark, Japan, Spain
   c. Canada, France, China, Russia
   d. Canada, Spain, China, Iceland

CRITICAL THINKING *Making Connections*

1. With a small group, discuss each of the ideas in the selection.
   Consider each of the following questions:

   • What are some advantages of these energy-saving ideas?
   • What are some disadvantages of these energy-saving ideas?
   • Which idea do you think would work in your community? Why do you think so?
   • How can you help save energy?
   • How could your school save energy?
2. Make your notes here.

_____

_____

_____

C **RESEARCHING** *Developing Research Questions*

1. Choose **one** source of energy mentioned in the selection, such as solar power, tidal power, wind, and so on. Research this source of energy further using the Internet or library resources.
2. Begin by developing a list of questions to focus your research. Your questions could include: How exactly does this energy form work? Who is using it? What problems are connected with it? What are its benefits?

> **TIPS**
>
> **Developing Research Questions**
> - Think about what you already know about the topic.
> - Think about what you want to know.
> - Remember the 5 Ws and H. (Who? Where? Why? When? What? How?)

D **VOCABULARY** *Words About Energy*

Use words from the selection to figure out these power clues.

1. This sweet export is burned to create electricity: __ __ __ __ __
2. Using fuels such as coal can cause this: __ __ __ __ __ __ __ __ __
3. France and Canada are using this source of electricity from the sea: __ __ __ __ __
4. This **E** word also means power: __ __ __ __ __ __
5. This source of electricity blows around the world: __ __ __ __ __
6. This fuel is cleaner and more efficient than fossil fuels: __ __ __ __ __ __ __ __
7. In Sweden, small cars run on this oil: __ __ __ __ __ __
8. This type of fuel is as old as the dinosaurs: __ __ __ __ __ __

E **WRITER'S CRAFT** *Alliteration*

> - **Alliteration** is the use of several words together that begin with the same sound. Writers use alliteration to create a certain effect that is pleasing to the reader's ear.
>   EXAMPLES: <u>w</u>ins <u>w</u>ith <u>w</u>ind   <u>f</u>reezes out <u>f</u>ossil <u>f</u>uels   <u>g</u>oes for <u>g</u>rains.

1. Find **one** more example of alliteration in the selection "Energy-Saving Ideas for a New World." Circle that example.
2. Rewrite **one** of the titles in this selection using alliteration.

Before Reading

Read the title and **by-line** (format and author's name) for this selection. Naya, the fictional character writing this diary, is a 15-year-old girl living on Earth in the year 2060, but looking forward to adventures on other planets. Read on to find out about Naya's life in the future.

During Reading

As you read, circle any words that you have never seen before, or words you know that are used in an unusual way. Try to work out their meaning by thinking about other words that they are like.

Life in 2060

Diary *by Catherine Rondina*

June 21, 2060

01   I haven't written much this month. I've been too busy with school, Civil Training Classes, and job training at the Air Garden. School was great this year. I passed all my subjects, barely. But what I liked this year was being in classes with other students, instead of just hooking up with kids and teachers through computers.

02   I got to know a lot of other teens my age and made some good friends. We play games, watch vids together, and go shopping and to the pool. Sometimes we even study together!

03   There's a great new 3-D video game that everyone is playing called *Invasion*. It's about aliens invading our solar system and the graphics on it really whirl. I've reached the thirteenth level but can't crack it any further.

04   Some of my classes were huge. My math class had over 300 students in it. I had a lot more tests and presentations this year, too.

GOALS AT A GLANCE

synthesizing information • making connections

05   I'm sort of glad we moved back to Earth, even if I miss
Neptune. Mom had such a cool job there testing all sorts of
new materials, but she says she's glad to be home, too.
I just don't know if I can get used to all the people here.
There's over 50 000 people in our Block. And it's really noisy,
all day and all night.

06   I have two weeks off before I leave for advanced tech
training on Pluto. I'll be helping to explore the planet, too,
as a Junior Scout. I can't wait to be away from home. Mom is
staying here, so I'll have my own mini-pod (4m x 4m x 4m,
with everything I need to live; the food delivered hot through
the pipes right to my "kitchen"). I can't wait!

07   Civil Training has been a lot tougher than I thought.
On our Block, there is a class with about 400 teenagers every
Saturday, all day. And then we have to volunteer five hours
a week.

08   I guess Civil Training is not so bad. Imagine what it was
like before war was banned 30 years ago. Mom says, when
she was a teenager, Civil Training included learning how to
fire a gun and patch up the wounded! That makes no sense!

09   Now there's peace, and teenagers can spend their four
Civil Training years helping in the community. My friend
Karine and I volunteer at a youth camp, which is a lot of fun.
We play a lot of old Earth games, like baseball and soccer.
As well, we help younger kids get their flying licences.

10   Job training at the Air Garden is a blast. I'm given
training and information on everything in the garden for
about two hours every day. And then for three hours every
day I have to walk around the gardens just talking to visitors
about the plants.

11   There are three garden spheres floating through our
Block, and they're always full of people walking around or
playing. It's really neat how these floating gardens work.
I have to use my PalmDetector to find out where the Air
Garden is each day, since it can move several kilometres
overnight. Then I take a helibus to the Air Garden.
When you look down on our Block from an Air Garden
the view is so cool.

12   In the Air Garden, all the plants grow in water. Sometimes I look at all the flowers and wonder what Earth looked like when there were plants and trees growing on the **ground**.

13   Tomorrow is Dad's sixtieth birthday. Dad's mother, who's 100, will be flying in from the Moon. We're having a big party for Dad at our Block's Recreation Pod. There'll be 50 people there so it will be crowded. It's a birthday **and** retirement party. I don't know how Dad is going to feel about not going to work every day, but the government makes everyone quit working at 60.

14   Meanwhile, the age to start working keeps increasing, since the number of jobs that **people** have to do keeps on decreasing. Robots and computers take over more and more jobs each year. Humans now have to be 30 to have a full-time job. Until then you go to school, or get job training, or tech training, or training in any other area you like.

15   Well, I'd better stop writing now. The pod light is dimming and everyone must go to bed. I hope they program a sunny day for tomorrow.

     Goodbye,

     Naya

A VOCABULARY *Determining Meaning*

1. What is the best meaning for the word **barely** as it is used in paragraph 1?
   a. easily   **b.** almost   **c.** only just   **d.** poorly

2. What is the best meaning for the word **banned** as it is used in paragraph 8?
   a. expelled   **b.** restricted   **c.** disqualified   **d.** forbidden

3. What is the best meaning for the word **wonder** as it is used in paragraph 12?
   a. speculate on   **b.** think about   **c.** question   **d.** marvel

4. What is the best meaning for the word **program** as it is used in paragraph 15?
   a. prepare for   **b.** a show   **c.** a schedule   **d.** arrange for

Answering Multiple-Choice Questions About Word Meaning

- Focus on the original sentence or paragraph.
- Ask yourself if you understand the word, sentence, or paragraph.
- Reread the sentence, replacing the word that is there with each of the new words that you are given.
- Cross out any new words that clearly don't fit the sentence.
- Think about which new word fits the sentence best.

B CRITICAL THINKING *Synthesizing Information*

For questions 1–3, your words can come from "Living in 2060" or from your reaction to the selection.

1. List **two** words to describe Naya's school life. _____ _____

2. List **two** words to describe Naya's life outside of school. _____ _____

3. List **two** words to describe homes in the year 2060. _____ _____

4. What do you think about the future described in this selection? In your notebook, create a Pro/Con chart like the one below. List at least **two** pros and **two** cons of this future, and include explanations for each point.

PRO	CON

EXTENDING: In your notebook, write a short description of the future based on this selection.

Compare your life with Naya's life. Use the following Venn diagram to help you. Consider categories such as home, family, school, work, entertainment, society, responsibilities, rights, and freedoms. If you need more room for your diagram, use another piece of paper.

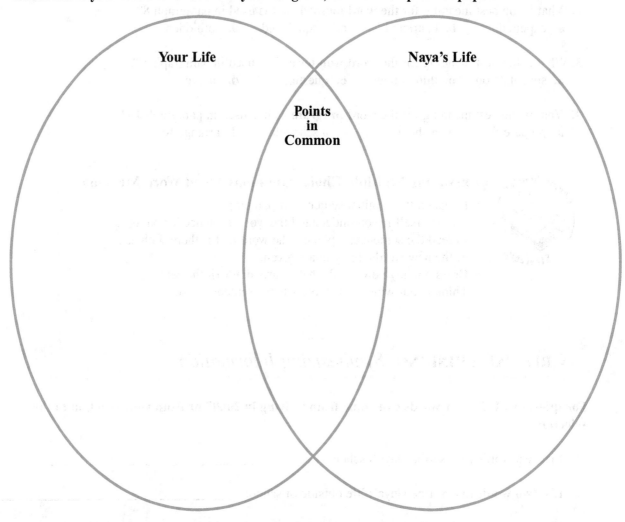

Your Life

Naya's Life

Points
in
Common

EXTENDING: Create a drawing that shows your life compared to Naya's life.

Making Connections

Making connections with a selection will increase your understanding and appreciation of it.
- Begin by thinking about your response to the selection.
- Think about how the selection reminds you of your own life.
- Then think about stories and people you are reminded of when you read the selection.
- Finally, return to your thoughts about the selection.
- Reflect on how your thoughts about the selection have been changed by this process.

- A **sentence** is a group of words that communicates a complete thought.
  EXAMPLE: Naya is worried about her Dad.

- An **incomplete sentence** does not communicate a complete thought. Information is missing.
  Quite often a noun, verb, or clause is missing.
  EXAMPLE: When Naya was worried about her Dad.

1. Some of the following are complete sentences, and some are not.
   Write **S** before each complete sentence. Write **I** before each incomplete sentence.

   _____ **a.** When the hockey season begins.

   _____ **b.** Last year I visited my cousin in New Brunswick.

   _____ **c.** On my way to school this morning.

   _____ **d.** "I like that new computer game," said Jonathan.

   _____ **e.** You're going to be late!

   _____ **f.** His mistake was an expensive one.

   _____ **g.** Please answer the telephone, Anna.

   _____ **h.** Hurrying to class.

   _____ **i.** What will you do now?

   _____ **j.** If you can't wait for me.

2. In your notebook, complete each incomplete sentence in question 1. You will need to invent the
   missing part of the sentence.

TIPS

Complete and Incomplete Sentences
- Using incomplete sentences can affect your meaning. If you're sending an
  important message and you need people to understand everything you're
  saying, then double-check that all your sentences are complete.

1. Choose **four** of the following words or phrases: **vids, helibus, Block, pod, mini-pod, Air Garden, PalmDetector, Civil Training**.
2. Use the Vocabulary Strategies below to help you work out the meaning of the four words you have chosen. Develop a definition for each of the four words as it might be used in the future. Write your definition in the space provided.

vids: _____

helibus: _____

Block: _____

pod: _____

mini-pod: _____

Air Garden: _____

PalmDetector: _____

Civil Training: _____

Reflecting

3. Did you have difficulty working out each word's meaning? Explain. _____

_____

_____

4. What do you think using these words added to the selection? _____

_____

_____

EXTENDING: Invent two more words to add to a "Future Dictionary." Include a definition.

_____

_____

Developing Meaning
- Scan the selection to find your four words.
- Reread the paragraphs where the new words are used.
- Think about how a new word has been used.
- Think about how the new words connect with words that you use every day.

UNIT 5 WRAP-UP

 SELF-ASSESSMENT *Comprehension Strategies*

1. Choose **one** item below. In your notebook, explain how you used this comprehension strategy, and how it improved your understanding of a selection.
   - ❑ retelling the story
   - ❑ forming questions about the selection
   - ❑ representing part of the story visually
   - ❑ representing the selection using graphic organizers
   - ❑ making connections between the selection, other selections, and your own experiences

2. Reflect on all the comprehension strategies you used in this unit. Based on your experiences, create a list of **five** comprehension tips that others could use.

 PROJECT IDEA *Visualizing the Future*

Think about the future suggested by this unit. These steps will help you communicate your ideas.

Step 1. Think about each selection you read in this unit. As a class, brainstorm ideas about what the world's future might be like.

Step 2. Complete this Venn diagram to compare the present with the future. Consider categories such as water use, energy, family, school, work, and society.

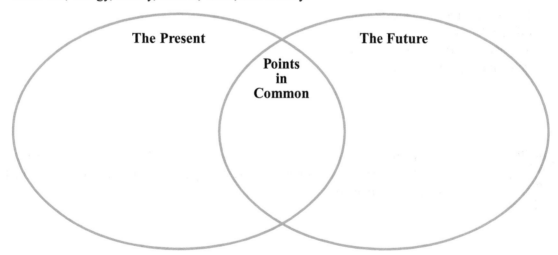

Step 3. Write at least **one** paragraph comparing the present with the future.

Step 4. Write at least **two** paragraphs explaining how you feel about life in the future. Include both pros and cons. Give your paragraphs a title.

TITLE
PARAGRAPH 1 Present and Future
PARAGRAPH 2 Pros of Life in the Future
PARAGRAPH 3 Cons of Life in the Future

Making connections means thinking about what you already know and how you feel about a subject, as well as thinking about other similar situations. Here's a process you can follow to help you make connections to a text.

Title

Ask Yourself: What clues does the title give me about the subject of the text? What ideas do I already have about the subject? What do I think the text will be about?

By-line

Ask Yourself: Have I read this type of text before? What can I expect from this text?

First paragraph

At this point, compare what is happening in this paragraph with things that have happened to you, to people you know, on TV shows you have watched, or in books you have read. Ask Yourself: How do I feel about the events in this text? What insights does the text give me?

Repeat this process as you read each paragraph of the text.

Living in 2060
Diary *by Catherine Rondina*

June 21, 2060

I haven't written much this month. I've been too busy with school, Civil Training Classes, and job training at the Air Garden. School was great this year. I passed all my subjects, barely. But what I liked this year was being in classes with other students, instead of just hooking up with kids and teachers through computers.

I got to know a lot of other teens my age and made some good friends. We play games, watch vids together, and go shopping and to the pool. Sometimes we even study together!

After reading the text, think about how it matters to you. How does this text change your views or attitudes? How does it make you feel? Try recording your response to the text in a personal journal or notebook.

Before Reading
"A Country Called Canada"

List **four rights** you think you have as a Canadian. Now, list **four responsibilities** you think you have as a Canadian.

Rights of Canadians	Responsibilities of Canadians
1.	1.
2.	2.
3.	3.
4.	4.

During Reading

An **editorial** gives an author's opinion on a topic. Facts or arguments are often used to support the author's opinion. As you read this editorial, keep the following questions in mind. After you've read the editorial, answer these questions.

What is the topic of this editorial?

What is the author's opinion?

What arguments support his point?

Do you agree or disagree? Explain why.

A Country Called Canada

Editorial *by Gary Lautens*

I have an idea.

Let's start a country.

This country would have bright leaders in politics, labour, business, education, and other fields.

They wouldn't squabble. They wouldn't call each other names.

They would try to get along.

In this country people would work hard—and they would be allowed to keep a lot of their money.

Oh, they'd help out the handicapped, the old, the sick, those who have been thrown out of work for no fault of their own.

But no <u>freeloading</u>.

You couldn't sit around twiddling your thumbs, abusing your body, making trouble, or just being a nuisance.

You would have to carry your share of the burden and not expect somebody else to always look after you.

You'd be responsible for your life—and no running away.

You'd have to be useful.

In this country you'd respect other people and they'd be expected to respect you. You could not sit around griping all the time or making a lot of demands.

If you made a mess of things, you'd be told to look for the <u>culprit</u> first in a mirror before you started pointing a finger.

You'd have to follow some rules because this country would work best that way.

GOALS AT A GLANCE

demonstrating understanding • comparing viewpoints

For example, you'd have to keep your mitts off other people, unless in affection. No abusing animals either, or property, or people's dreams.

You'd be asked to understand things like feelings and hopes.

Kids?

In this country kids would be special and need a lot of love and peanut butter sandwiches and talks. In return, they'd be expected to go to school, learn something useful and not be smart alecks.

They could keep pets provided they looked after them.

You'd be expected to cherish this country and treat it kindly. You'd be expected to understand its riches—and make sure something was left for the next generation.

And no putting it in second place to another country.

You can get sentimental about some holiday place, or a country in your past, or something you saw in *National Geographic*.

Of course, it's permissible to get dreamy about Paris, too. Everyone does.

But this country would be top priority, Number 1, your very own place, home.

You'd feel good about other people from your own country, even if they were a little different. You wouldn't act like a goof and insult them or treat them in a way you wouldn't want to be treated.

This country would have a nice touch of pride—but pride in important things like <u>integrity</u>, intelligence, cleanliness, decency, and being fair. It wouldn't get a big head about things that are just luck.

What else?

I think I've left out fun.

This country should have lots of fun because life isn't much without it. You wouldn't want a country where everyone has a long face and snaps about the littlest thing.

You'd want to hear laughter. It's about as important as sunshine.

No <u>idlers</u>. No bullies. No grouches. No <u>ingrates</u>. No shouters. No sourpusses. No crybabies. No <u>parasites</u>. No hotheads.

Yes, let's start a country.

We could call it Canada.

VOCABULARY

integrity: moral correctness, uncorrupted

idlers: lazy people

ingrates: ungrateful people

parasites: people who live off the work of others, another word for **freeloaders**

Write <u>true</u> or <u>false</u> after each statement below.

1. Gary Lautens believes a country should not have bright leaders in politics. _____

2. Lautens thinks that every citizen should be useful. _____

3. Lautens wants people to be responsible for their actions. _____

4. He does not think rules are a good idea. _____

5. Lautens wants kids to be smart alecks. _____

6. Lautens does not think it is necessary for people to have fun. _____

7. Lautens believes that Canada is already like the country he describes. _____

B **CRITICAL THINKING** *Comparing Viewpoints*

1. Explain what Lautens would like to see Canada become.

   _____
   _____
   _____

2. Now, explain how you feel about Lautens' ideas and viewpoints.

   _____
   _____
   _____

3. What do you think Canada should be like? List at least **four** ideas.

   _____
   _____
   _____
   _____

4. Why do you think Lautens uses short, choppy sentences and short paragraphs in his editorial? What effect does this have on the reader?

   _____
   _____

C   VISUAL COMMUNICATION *Collage*

1. Choose **one** idea from this selection that you feel strongly about.
2. Find drawings or photos that represent this idea. These images should also represent your position (for or against the idea).
3. Find headlines, slogans, or other bits of text that connect with the idea.
4. Arrange these items in a **collage**.
5. Give your collage a good title.

> A **collage** is a picture made by arranging items with different textures, colours, and shapes on a background. You can use images and print texts to create your collage.

D   VOCABULARY *Using Roots to Work Out Meaning*

- A **root** is a word or part of a word that can be used to form other words.

  EXAMPLES: free<u>load</u>ing   loader   unload   reload
                root

- A good strategy for working out the meaning of some words is to look at the root of the word. If you can figure out the root word, you may be able to figure out the meaning of the whole word.

- For example, Lautens uses the word **permissible**. You may recognize that the first part of this word is **perm**, and that might remind you of the word **permission**. If you know that the word **permission** means "to allow," you will be able to figure out that **permissible** is a similar word meaning "it's allowed."

1. <u>Underline</u> the **root** word of each word listed below.

   a. useful _____

   b. kindly _____

   c. dreamy _____

   d. different _____

   e. cleanliness _____

   f. littlest _____

   g. laughter _____

   h. idlers _____

2. For each word in question 1, think of another word with the same root. Write your word in the blank space provided above.

- A **synonym** is a word with the same or similar meaning to another word. For example, <u>tell</u>, <u>advise</u>, <u>inform</u>, and <u>notify</u> are synonyms. They all mean roughly the same thing.

- Good writers choose words carefully to create variety in their writing and to have a certain effect on a reader. Sometimes, this means considering other synonyms. For example, Lautens uses the word **culprit**, when he could have used the synonym **guilty party**. He chose the word **culprit** for the effect it would have on the reader.

- You can use a **thesaurus** to find synonyms for most common words. Be careful when you're choosing synonyms. The connotation, and even the meaning, of synonyms may vary from the original word, so the meaning or effect of your sentence might change. Use a dictionary to check the meaning of your synonym to make sure you are still saying what you want to say.

1. Give **one** synonym for each <u>underlined</u> word in the following sentences. Choose a synonym that makes sense and does not change the meaning of the sentence. Check a thesaurus if you need help.

   a. This country would have <u>bright</u> leaders. _____

   b. People would work <u>hard</u>. _____

   c. You'd have to be <u>useful</u>. _____

   d. Get <u>dreamy</u> about Paris. _____

   e. You wouldn't <u>act</u> like a goof. _____

   f. You could <u>call</u> it Canada. _____

2. Using the synonyms you found for question 1, write a short paragraph about the Canada you would like to see.

   _____

   _____

   _____

   _____

   _____

Choosing Synonyms

- Use synonyms to replace overused or tired words (like <u>said</u> or <u>nice</u>).
- Choose synonyms with different connotations or slightly different meanings to create certain effects (like <u>whimper</u>, <u>cry</u>, <u>snivel</u>, or <u>bawl</u>).
- Check that the new word works in the sentence.
- Make sure that you understand the meaning of the synonym.

Before Reading

During the 1960s in the United States, many people fought for civil rights and equality. Black Americans faced racism, hatred, abuse, and murder. This poem is about the bombing of a church in Birmingham, Alabama in 1963.

Ballad of Birmingham

Poem *by Dudley Randall*

"Mother dear, may I go downtown
instead of out to play,
and march the streets of Birmingham
in a freedom march today?"

"No baby, no, you may not go,
for the dogs are fierce and wild,
and clubs and hoses, guns and jails
ain't good for a little child."

"But, mother, I won't be alone.
Other children will go with me,
and march the streets of Birmingham
to make our country free."

"No, baby, no, you may not go,
for I fear those guns will fire.
But you may go to church instead
and sing in the children's choir."

She has combed and brushed her nightdark hair,
and bathed rose-petal sweet,
and drawn white gloves on her small brown hands,
and white shoes on her feet.

The mother smiled to know her child
was in the sacred place,
but that smile was the last smile
to come upon her face.

For when she heard the explosion,
her eyes grew wet and wild.
She raced through the streets of Birmingham
calling for her child.

She clawed through bits of glass and brick,
then lifted out a shoe.
"O, here's the shoe my baby wore,
but, baby, where are you?"

VOCABULARY

ain't: slang for "are not"

GOALS AT A GLANCE

finding the main idea • summarizing the poem

A UNDERSTANDING THE SELECTION *Finding the Main Ideas*

1. Read each sentence below. Circle the **three** main ideas from "Ballad of Birmingham."

   a. The mother is frightened her child will be harmed if she goes to the freedom march.

   b. The child must look nice before she goes to church.

   c. The mother feels her child will be safe at church.

   d. The child must wear white shoes to church.

   e. Birmingham is not a good place for children.

   f. Hatred cannot be escaped in church.

2. What is the hardest part about finding the main ideas of a poem?
   What reading strategies helped you?

   _____

   _____

B CRITICAL THINKING *Summarizing*

For each <u>stanza</u> (group of four lines) of the poem, write one sentence that explains (or <u>summarizes</u>) what is happening. Stanza 1 has been done for you.

Stanza 1: _A child asks her mother if she can join a freedom march, a protest against racism._

Stanza 2: _____

Stanza 3: _____

Stanza 4: _____

Stanza 5: _____

Stanza 6: _____

Stanza 7: _____

Stanza 8: _____

Summarizing

- To **summarize** is to make a brief statement giving the main points of a text.
- Read each stanza several times until you are sure you know what is happening in it.
- Rewrite each stanza in plain language, recording what has happened.
- Reread your answers and think about the events in the poem.

VISUAL COMMUNICATION *Illustrating a Stanza*

1. Choose one stanza from the poem and draw an illustration for it.
2. Begin by listing the details your drawing will include.

_____

_____

_____

_____

D

WRITER'S CRAFT *Descriptive Words*

- **Descriptive words** can bring an image to life. They can help you visualize what you are reading.

  EXAMPLES FROM THE POEM: <u>nightdark</u> hair   <u>rose-petal</u> sweet

1. Think of **one** word to describe each of the following things.

   a. fire _____

   b. bomb _____

   c. explosion _____

   d. eyes _____

   e. smile _____

   f. shoes _____

   g. mother _____

   h. father _____

   i. child _____

   j. house _____

2. Now, add one more word for each word in question 1.

What can you do when someone you love is hurt or murdered during a crime? Think about this question as you read "Virginie's Story." Find out what one young woman did when her sister died.

Virginie's Story

Magazine Article *by Max Paris from* Adbusters Magazine

Here are a couple of violent scenes:

> **Scene One**: A young girl is walking back to her relative's house after buying bread at the store. On her way back she is attacked by a man who robs her of six dollars and then kills her.

> **Scene Two**: A police officer catches a suspected criminal. He throws him to the ground, places his foot on the suspect's chest, and levels a shotgun at his head.

Both of these scenes could easily be shown on TV. Scene Two is a movie trailer for a Bruce Willis action flick. Scene One is what happened to Virginie Lariviere's sister, Marie-Eve, a real-life violent scene.

Experts debate the connections between real-life violence and that on TV, but for Virginie, there is no debate. "My sister and I liked to watch violent movies like *Terminator* and *Robocop*, and I thought that might have something to do with her murder," Virginie declares. "I was so mad my sister was killed. I had to do something."

What did she do? She created a petition, asking for support in her campaign against violence. While the petition was circulating she made speaking appearances on TV, radio, and at media conferences all over the country to announce her campaign. Finally, in November 1992, Virginie presented then Prime Minister Brian Mulroney with the signatures of 1.3 million Canadians who believed, like her, that there was far too much violence on TV.

To other activist-minded teens, Virginie offers this advice: "Do what you believe in. And always follow your convictions, no matter what your cause."

GOALS AT A GLANCE

making judgments • TV violence tally

A UNDERSTANDING THE SELECTION *Recalling Details*

1. a. What happened to Virginie Lariviere's sister? _____

_____

b. What did Virginie do in response to what happened to her sister? _____

_____

_____

2. a. What do "experts debate," according to this article? _____

_____

b. How did Virginie feel about this debate? _____

_____

3. What advice does Virginie give to teenagers who want to take action? _____

_____

_____

B CRITICAL THINKING *Making Judgments*

1. a. What do you think of Virginie's actions? _____

_____

b. What would you have done in her place? _____

_____

2. How do you think Virginie Lariviere felt once her petition was presented to the prime minister?

_____

3. How effective do you think a petition against TV violence would be? Explain. _____

_____

4. a. Why do you think the author, Max Paris, begins the article by presenting two scenes?

_____

b. How effective do you think this beginning is? _____

_____

C. ORAL COMMUNICATION *Informal Debate*

1. Do you think there's too much violence on TV? Do you think TV violence can cause an increase in violence in real life? Get together with a small group of students to discuss these questions.
2. Present your ideas and feelings to the group.
3. Listen carefully as others tell you their ideas and feelings.
4. Respond to these ideas and feelings.

EXTENDING: In your notebook, write a paragraph explaining your response to the questions about TV violence in question 1. Include the opinions of others and your response to these opinions.

D. MEDIA *TV Violence Tally*

1. The next time you watch TV, record the number of violent acts you see in a two-hour period.
2. For each act of violence you see, place an **X** in the correct column and correct row on the following chart.

Types of Violence	News	Sitcom	Drama	Sports	Other
Verbal Abuse (people yelling at each other or name-calling)					
Physical Abuse (people fighting but not getting seriously injured)					
Extreme Violence (leading to serious injury or death)					

3. Discuss your chart with your class. What conclusions can you reach about violence on TV?

_____

_____

_____

Reflecting
?

4. Did creating the chart change your ideas or opinions about TV violence? If so, explain how.

_____

_____

_____

Before Reading

When you watch police shows on TV, what do you expect to see?

_____

_____

_____

Law and *Dis*order

TV Scene *by Dee-Lynne Scott*

Anna Ludwinski (undercover detective)

Tom Hepburn (undercover detective)

Kim Yeung (junior police officer)

Dr. Sing (witness)

Ms. Groundwood (store owner)

Setting: Small, rural town. Present day.
It's early morning, raining.

Characters: Anna Ludwinski, undercover detective
Tom Hepburn, undercover detective
Kim Yeung, junior police officer
Dr. Sing, local doctor, witness
Ms. Groundwood, store owner

Opening Scene: A bicycle store has been broken into.
The detectives, Anna and Tom, have just
arrived on the scene. Crime tape surrounds
a broken window.

* * * *

Anna: *(to Kim)* What have we got here?

Kim: *(referring to her notepad)* Bicycle store broken into at
4:45 a.m. Alarm sounded, bringing Ms. Groundwood to the
scene. Dr. Sing, who was walking his dog at the time, saw a
large man escaping from the scene on a new, expensive bike.

Tom: *(looking around)* Well, have you dusted for prints?

Kim: Yes, sir. But it's a busy store. And Ms. Groundwood
says nothing is missing, except for the one bike.

Ms. Groundwood: Yes, just the one bike. I don't keep any
money in the store at night.

Anna: There's quite a bit of damage, though.

> **GOALS AT A GLANCE**
>
> analysing characters • writing dialogue

Ms. Groundwood: Yes, the window alone will cost $1000 to replace. And a display case was smashed as well.

Tom: *(closing his notebook)* Sounds like the work of local teens! These kids, always causing trouble.

Anna: *(glaring at him)* Tom, you're stereotyping teenagers again. There are plenty of great kids in this town. And troublemakers come in all ages. This looks to me like the work of Pedals Jones. He's struck three other stores in the area.

Ms. Groundwood: Right. I've heard about those cases.

Dr. Sing: So have I. If you know it's this Pedals Jones, why don't you arrest him?

Anna: Pedals Jones is just what we've been **calling** the thief. We really don't know who he is. It might even be a woman. This is the first of the four stores where there's been a witness who actually saw someone.

Tom: There's no connection between these cases!

Anna: *(sarcastically)* Sure! At every store it's been an early morning burglary, a broken window, no prints, and one missing bike.

Tom: But other than that…

Anna: *(speaking over Tom's protests)* Ms. Groundwood, we'll file a report and you'll be able to contact your insurance company tomorrow morning. Officer Yeung can help you get your shop boarded up for now. *(Ms. Groundwood and Kim move off)* Dr. Sing, thank you very much for your time. We would like to talk with you further. You're our first witness, and I think you have some valuable information that will help us finally catch this thief.

Tom: Sure, sure! Whatever. But now I'll just go and question some of the local teenagers; see what they were up to last night.

Anna: Tom! Have you ever heard the expression "innocent until proven guilty"?

Tom: Sure, I hear that all the time: from the guilty!

(Camera fades to commercial)

Write true or false after each statement below.

1. The crime scene is located in a big city. _____

2. Kim Yeung is an undercover detective. _____

3. A candy store has been broken into. _____

4. Dr. Sing is the only witness. _____

5. Ms. Groundwood owns the store that was broken into. _____

6. There is less than $100 of damage to the store. _____

7. Tom Hepburn stereotypes teenagers as troublemakers. _____

8. Kim agrees with Tom. _____

9. Anna thinks the burglary might be the work of Pedals Jones. _____

10. The burglaries of the four stores all have elements in common. _____

B **CRITICAL THINKING** *Analysing Characters*

1. In this short scene, the reader is given some information about Tom and Anna.
   For each character, list **three** words to describe him or her.

Tom	Anna

2. Given your understanding of each character, list **two** ideas about what will happen in the next scene.

_____

_____

C WRITING *Dialogue*

1. This selection is the first scene in a show about two detectives who are constantly arguing with each other. What will Anna and Tom do next? Return to your ideas for activity B, question 2, and your response to the question at the beginning of the selection.
2. Write the second scene between these two characters. Writing with a partner may help you.
3. Give some clues about how the crime will be solved.
4. Use another sheet of paper if you need more space or if you want to add other characters to the scene.

SETTING: _____

Anna: _____

Tom: _____

Anna: _____

Tom: _____

Anna: _____

Tom: _____

Anna: _____

Tom: _____

Anna: _____

Tom: _____

Anna: _____

Tom: _____

D MEDIA *Analysing Media Texts*

1. Think about a police show (or comic book or movie about the police) that you enjoy. Answer each question below in your notebook:
   - What is the name of the show?
   - What is the setting for this show?
   - What are the characters like?
   - Are the characters believable? Explain.
   - Why do you enjoy watching this show?
   - Give one reason why you would recommend this show to a friend.
2. Discuss your answers with a small group.

Before Reading

Read the title for the short story and think about the following definition of **alias**.

> **alias:** also known as; with the assumed name of: <u>Jane Smith,</u>
> <u>alias Jane Happy, was wanted in all ten provinces for fraud.</u>

O. Henry got the idea for the story "Alias Jimmy Valentine" when he was in prison. A fellow prisoner suggested the idea for this story about a reformed safe-cracker named Jimmy Valentine. "Alias Jimmy Valentine" is set in the United States in the early 1900s.

Alias Jimmy Valentine

Short Story *by O. Henry*

A guard came to the prison shoe shop, where Jimmy Valentine had been working for the ten months of his stay.

"Warden wants you in the front office," said the guard, taking Jimmy's arm. "Looks like you've got your pardon from the governor."

"About time," said Jimmy.

A man with as many friends "on the outside" as Jimmy Valentine had was never in prison for long. Ten months was the most time he'd ever done.

The warden didn't hand him the pardon right away. As always, he gave him strong words of advice first.

"You'll go out in the morning, Valentine, and this time I want you to make an honest man of yourself. You're not a bad fellow at heart. Just stop cracking safes, and go straight."

"Me?" said Jimmy, in surprise. "Why, I never cracked a safe in my life."

The warden laughed.

"Oh no. Of course not. Then how come you got sent up on that Springfield job? Was it just a mean old jury that had it in for you?"

"Me?" Jimmy kept on looking surprised. "Why, warden, I never was in Springfield in all my life!"

"Take him back, guard," said the warden, "and fix him up with a new suit and shoes. Have him in my office at seven in the morning. And Valentine: better think over my advice."

ASK YOURSELF
What is your opinion of Jimmy Valentine's character?

* * * * * *

At quarter past seven next morning, Jimmy stood in the warden's office. He had on a cheap, shiny, badly fitting suit. On his feet were stiff, squeaky shoes.

The warden gave him a railroad ticket, a five-dollar bill, a cheap cigar, and a handshake. He also gave him yesterday's advice all over again, and wished him luck.

Mr. James Valentine, no longer Prisoner Number 9762, walked out into the sunshine.

Not even glancing at the trees, the birds, the flowers, Jimmy went right to the nearest restaurant and had the biggest breakfast he'd had in ten months. He finished it off with a far better cigar than the warden had given him.

ASK YOURSELF
Do you think Jimmy will follow the warden's advice? Why or why not?

* * * * * *

Then he walked to the railroad station and boarded a train.

Within three hours, he was in a little town near the state line. He went at once to a bar owned by an old pal, Mike Dolan. The two shook hands.

"Sorry we couldn't make it sooner, Jimmy," said Mike, "but the governor was a tough one. How are you?"

"Fine," said Jimmy. "Got my key?"

He got his key and went upstairs, unlocking the door of a room at the rear.

Everything was just as he had left it, even the collar button on the floor, the one he had yanked from the shirt of Detective Ben Price, the man who had come to arrest him.

From the back of the closet, Jimmy pulled his dusty old suitcase. He opened it and stood staring happily at the finest set of safecracker's tools anywhere in the Midwest.

There were drills, punches, braces, clamps, even a few special pieces designed by Jimmy himself. The whole set was worth nearly a thousand dollars.

When he went downstairs again, Jimmy was dressed in a handsome, well-fitting suit. He was carrying his cleaned, dusted suitcase.

"What's up this time, Jimmy?" Mike wanted to know. "Got anything in mind?"

"Me?" Jimmy looked surprised. "Just off to do an honest day's work, Mike. I'm the new sales manager for the finest cookie and biscuit company in the Midwest."

Mike laughed so hard he nearly dropped the glass he was drying.

* * * * * *

A week after the release of Prisoner Number 9762, three safe burglaries were reported to the police. Not a clue was left to any of them, except that they were all done in the same manner.

"That's Jimmy Valentine," declared Ben Price.

He knew Jimmy's habits. The jobs were clean, neat, easy.

No more than one hole had to be drilled for any of them. No trace of the burglar was ever left behind.

"He'll do his full sentence this time," vowed Ben. "No more pardons for Jimmy Valentine!"

* * * * * *

One afternoon, Jimmy climbed off the train in a small town called Elmore, carrying his heavy suitcase. He looked so handsome in his fine new suit, he might have been a college student home for a visit.

A lovely young lady crossed the street, passed him at the corner, and walked up the steps of the Elmore Bank.

Jimmy Valentine took one look at her, forgot who he was, and became a new man.

Shyly, the young lady returned his glance. Young men of Jimmy's style and good looks were scarce in Elmore. Then she looked quickly away and hurried into the bank.

A little boy was loafing on the steps. Jimmy tossed him a dime.

"Beg pardon," he said, "but wasn't that, um, Miss Polly Simpson that just went into the bank?"

"Nope," said the boy, "but I know who it is. Got another dime?"

Three dimes later, Jimmy found out that the lady was Miss Annabel Adams. Three more dimes and he knew that she was the bank owner's daughter.

Jimmy Valentine, the new man, needed a new name. At the local hotel, he signed in as Mr. Ralph D. Spencer.

He also needed a new means of earning a living. There was only one thing he knew as much about as safecracking.

ASK YOURSELF
Why does Ben make this vow?

"I'm planning to settle in Elmore," he told the hotel clerk. "I was thinking about opening a shoe store. Are there any others in town?"

"Not a one," said the clerk. "We could really use a good shoe store. I'm sure you'll be a success, Mr. Spencer."

ASK YOURSELF
Why does Jimmy decide to open a shoe store?

* * * * * *

Mr. Spencer was a success. The shoe store did well from the start, as did its handsome, charming owner. Soon he had many friends in Elmore. Among these was Miss Annabel Adams.

At the end of a year, the two were engaged to be married. Mr. Ralph D. Spencer was warmly welcomed into the Adams family.

One day Jimmy sat down and wrote a letter to an old friend in St. Louis.

"Dear Billy," the letter read, "I have a gift for you. I want you to have my kit of tools. I have no need for them now. I'm going to marry the finest girl in the world in two weeks. She believes in me, Billy, and I wouldn't do another crooked thing for the world. Meet me in Sully's Bar on Tuesday night. I'll have the tools with me. Your old pal, Jimmy."

On the very day he wrote this letter, Ben Price came to Elmore. From the drugstore across the street from Spencer's Shoe Store, he got a good look at its owner, Mr. Ralph D. Spencer.

"Aha!" said Ben to himself. "Marry the banker's daughter, will you, Jimmy Valentine? We'll see about that!"

* * * * * *

On Tuesday morning, when Jimmy was to leave for St. Louis, Annabel's father asked him to stop off at the bank for a moment, along with the rest of the Adams family. He wanted to show off to them all his brand-new bank vault.

They were a large, happy party: Annabel, her married sister and two small daughters, Mr. Ralph D. Spencer, and Mr. Adams.

Laughing and talking as they went into the bank, they didn't notice Ben Price. His back turned to them, he was leaning against a wall outside the room they were entering.

The shiny new vault was a marvel, with a time-lock that had to be turned this way and that to make the heavy door close.

Since the vault was not yet in use, the door stood open now. The little girls were more interested than anybody. They looked inside, listening and watching as Mr. Adams explained its workings.

And then, all in a moment, the bigger girl playfully
pushed her little sister inside and slammed the door shut.
She turned the knob, just as she had seen Mr. Adams do.
Then she smiled, proud of what she had done.

Inside the vault, her sister screamed in terror.

Mr. Adams was terrified, too. So was the child's mother,
and everyone else in the room.

"I can't open the door!" cried Mr. Adams, pulling at the
handle just the same. "The time-lock hasn't been set yet!
There isn't a man nearer than a hundred miles from here who
can do it! And there isn't much air in that vault!"

* * * * * *

Ask Yourself
What will happen next?

"Oh, Ralph!" Suddenly Annabel was pulling at the
sleeve of the man she loved, certain that he, above all men
on earth, would be the one to perform a miracle. "Oh, Ralph,
isn't there something you can do?"

He looked at her with a strange smile on his lips.
All at once, Mr. Ralph D. Spencer was gone from the room.
In his place stood Jimmy Valentine.

In a flash, he threw off his coat. Then he set his heavy
suitcase on a table and opened it. He took out his tools, one
by one, and set them out.

Then he went silently to work. In a minute his pet drill
was biting into the heavy door. Within a few minutes more,
breaking his own speed record, Jimmy opened the door.

The frightened child, unharmed, fell into her mother's
arms.

* * * * * *

Ask Yourself
Has Jimmy just become a hero or a
safecracker?

Jimmy Valentine put on his coat, packed up his tools,
and walked to the front door. As he went, he thought he heard
a faraway voice that he once knew calling out "Ralph! Oh,
Ralph!" but he never stopped walking.

At the door, a big man stood in his way.

"Hello, Ben," said Jimmy, still smiling his odd, sad smile.
"Here at last, are you? Well, let's go. Can't see that it makes
much difference now."

And then Ben Price said a strange thing.

"You must be mistaken, sir. I don't believe I know you."

Without another look, he turned away and strolled down
the street.

Ask Yourself
Why does Ben pretend not to know
Jimmy?

Alias Jimmy Valentine   **147**

A UNDERSTANDING THE SELECTION *Recalling Details*

Underline the correct ending for each sentence.

1. Jimmy got his pardon from the governor and got out of jail because he (was innocent / had friends on the outside / was the governor's brother).

2. The warden told Jimmy to stop cracking (secret codes / safes / his knuckles).

3. Jimmy Valentine's new name was Mr. (Ralph D. Spencer / Ronald D. Spoony / Steven R. Valentine).

4. Annabel's father wanted to show off his new (plans / building / vault).

5. Ben Price pretended he (was a bank robber / was not a police officer / didn't know Jimmy).

B CRITICAL THINKING *Evaluating the Story*

You can use point form to answer these questions.

1. What will happen to Jimmy Valentine now? _____

_____

_____

2. Are the choices Jimmy makes throughout the story good choices? Explain. _____

_____

_____

3. Do the characters in this story behave in a believable way? Explain. _____

_____

_____

4. Was there anything in this story that surprised you? Explain. _____

_____

_____

5. Why do you think the author called his story "Alias Jimmy Valentine" and not "Alias Ralph D. Spencer"?

_____

_____

EXTENDING: In your response journal, explain what you liked and did not like about this story.

C ORAL COMMUNICATION *Retell the Story*

1. Make notes of each of the main events in "Alias Jimmy Valentine."
2. Retell the story to a partner.
3. Listen as your partner retells the story to you. Add any details your partner leaves out.
4. Compare your retelling of the story with your partner's retelling. Can you explain any differences?

_____

_____

D WRITING *A Letter*

1. Reread Jimmy Valentine's letter to Billy.
2. Think about what Jimmy tells his friend.
3. In the space below, write a letter to a friend you have not seen for a long time.
4. Describe some of the recent events in your life.

(Date) _____

(Greeting) _____ ,

(Message) _____

_____

_____

_____

_____

(Closing) _____

(Signature) _____

Letters

Find the letter Jimmy writes to his friend (page 146).
On it **circle** each of the following letter features:
- **greeting**: letters always begin with a greeting, such as "Dear Jimmy," (Many letters also include the **date** at the top.)
- **message**: after the greeting comes what you want to tell the person
- **closing**: a polite ending, such as "Your friend," or "Sincerely,"
- **signature**: the name of the person sending the letter

1. A good writer can reveal what a character is like through how the character speaks. Reread the following dialogue from the story:

> "Warden wants you in the front office," said the guard, taking Jimmy's arm. "Looks like you've got your pardon from the governor."
> "About time," said Jimmy.
> A man with as many friends "on the outside" as Jimmy Valentine had was never in prison for long. Ten months was the most time he'd ever done.
> The warden didn't hand him the pardon right away. As always, he gave him strong words of advice first.
> "You'll go out in the morning, Valentine, and this time I want you to make an honest man of yourself. You're not a bad fellow at heart. Just stop cracking safes, and go straight."
> "Me?" said Jimmy, in surprise. "Why, I never cracked a safe in my life."
> The warden laughed.
> "Oh no. Of course not. Then how come you got sent up on that Springfield job? Was it just a mean old jury that had it in for you?"
> "Me?" Jimmy kept on looking surprised. "Why, warden, I never was in Springfield in all my life!"
> "Take him back, guard," said the warden, "and fix him up with a new suit and shoes. Have him in my office at seven in the morning. And Valentine: better think over my advice."

2. List **two** things you learn about Jimmy Valentine from what Jimmy says.

_____

_____

_____

3. List **two** things you learn about Jimmy from what the warden says.

_____

_____

4. List **two** things you learn about the warden from what the warden says.

_____

_____

5. How skilled do you think you are at picking up the clues an author gives you about a character? How do you think you could improve your skills?

_____

_____

UNIT 6 WRAP-UP

SELF-ASSESSMENT *Critical Thinking Strategies*

1. In your notebook, explain how you used at least **three** of the following critical thinking strategies. How did they improve your understanding of a selection?
   - ❏ comparing viewpoints
   - ❏ finding the main ideas
   - ❏ summarizing
   - ❏ making judgments
   - ❏ analysing characters
   - ❏ evaluating the story

2. Set a personal goal for using and improving your use of the above strategies. Explain what you will do.

_____

_____

PROJECT IDEA *Informal Debate*

Debate one of the issues raised in this unit.

Step 1. Think about each selection you read in this unit. Choose **one** of the following topics as a focus for an informal debate:
   - ❏ what makes a country great
   - ❏ equal rights for everyone
   - ❏ justice for victims and the family of victims
   - ❏ stereotyping teenagers or others
   - ❏ the modern justice system

Step 2. Jot down notes for at least **four** points you want to make. Be ready to support your points with facts or arguments.

_____

_____

_____

Step 3. Discuss your points with a partner who has chosen the same topic. Take turns presenting each point. Present your first point clearly, and then listen to any comments your partner makes about that point. Your partner will then present his or her first point, and you need to listen and respond to it before moving on to your next point.

Step 4. Has the debating process **confirmed** or **changed** (choose **one**) your thoughts on the topic? Explain why.

_____

_____

Trying to <u>summarize</u> a text can increase your understanding of it. Here's a process you can follow as you create a summary of a text.

Selection
Reread **all** of the selection. Make sure you understand it. If you're confused, discuss the selection with another classmate or your teacher.

Paragraphs or Sections
Focus on one paragraph or section of text at a time. You may need to break up the text into **meaningful chunks**, sections of text that seem to be about the same thing. For example, this section is all about leaders.

Main Ideas
Think about the main idea of each section of text. It may help to highlight or underline the main idea. For example, in the above section, the main ideas are <u>bright leaders</u> and <u>get along</u>.

A Country Called Canada
Editorial *by Gary Lautens*

I have an idea.

Let's start a country.

This country would have <u>bright leaders</u> in politics, labour, business, education, and other fields.

They wouldn't squabble. They wouldn't call each other names.

They would try to <u>get along</u>.

In this country people would work hard—and they would be allowed to keep a lot of their money.

Summarize Using Your Own Words
Reword the main idea in your own words. For example, <u>a good country would have intelligent leaders that work together</u> is the main idea of the section identified in Paragraphs or Sections.

Setting Goals
How good are you at summarizing texts? How could you improve your use of this skill? Set a goal for improving your use of summarizing in the next month.

_____

_____

_____

5 Ws and H: Who? Where? Why? When? What? and How? are the questions every newspaper article should answer

abbreviation: the short form of a word or words (for example, Thurs., Sept., B.C.)

adjective: a word that describes a noun or a pronoun (for example, great, red, smooth)

adverb: a word that modifies a verb. It tells the reader more about the action (for example, slowly, brightly)

alliteration: the use of several words together that begin with the same sound (for example, the wind whistled without resting)

audience: the people who will be reading your writing

by-line: in a selection, the information beneath the title that tells you who wrote or created the piece and what its format is

caption: the description beside or beneath a photo or illustration telling you about the image

comma: a punctuation mark (,) that separates elements in a sentence and tells the reader to pause

command: a statement or phrase that orders you to do something

comparative: the second degree of comparison of adjectives and adverbs, usually formed by adding **-er** to the end of the word, or using the word **more** (for example, quicker, more slowly)

cons: disadvantages (as in "pros and cons")

conjunction: a word (for example, and, but, because) that is used to join words or groups of words

descriptive words: words that can bring an image to life and create pictures in the reader's mind

design: the use of colour, the placement of images and words, and text type on a page

dialogue: the words characters speak to each other

editorial: a piece of writing that gives an author's opinion on a topic

exclamation: a sentence or phrase that expresses strong feelings

exclamation mark: a punctuation mark (!) that shows a sentence is an exclamation

fine print: the small print at the bottom of an ad

headline: the title of an article

homophone: a word that sounds the same as another word or words, but has a different meaning and a different spelling (for example, its, it's)

incomplete sentence: a sentence that does not express a complete thought and is missing either the subject or the verb

KWL chart: a chart recording what you **K**now, **W**ant to Know, and have **L**earned

message: the information or idea a writer is trying to give the reader

noun: a word that names a person, place, thing, quality, or event

past tense: the verb tense used to tell about something that happened in the past

period: a punctuation mark (.) that ends a statement or command

plural noun: a noun that names more than one person, place, thing, quality, or event

predict: to make an educated guess about what will happen

present tense: the verb tense that is used to tell what is happening now, or that an action is ongoing

prefix: the part of a word added to the beginning of a root word to change its meaning (for example, <u>un</u>happy, <u>non</u>-smoker)

profile: a short description of a person's character or career

pros: advantages (as in "pros and cons")

purpose: the reason a text was created (for example, to persuade someone to do or buy something)

question: a sentence or phrase that asks something

question mark: the punctuation mark (?) used to end a question

quotation marks: punctuation marks (" ") that are used to show that someone is speaking

retell: to tell something to someone in a different way

root: a word or part of a word that can be used to form other words (for example, un<u>happy</u>, im<u>puls</u>ive)

sense words: words that describe how something looks, sounds, feels, smells, or tastes

sentence: a group of words that expresses a complete thought

similes: a phrase that compares one thing to another using the words **like, than,** or **as** (for example, the wind cut through me <u>like a knife</u>)

singular noun: a noun that names one person, place, thing, quality, or event

skim: to quickly read parts of a text to get a sense of what it is about

slogan: a short, easy-to-remember message

speech tag: words that come before or after dialogue and show who has spoken

stanza: a group of lines in a poem

statement: a sentence or phrase that tells you something

suffix: the part of a word that is added to the end of a root word to change its meaning (for example, joy<u>ful</u>, wolf<u>ish</u>)

superlative: the third degree of comparison of adjectives and adverbs, usually formed by adding **-est** to a word, or using the word **most** (for example, quick<u>est</u>, <u>most fun</u>)

synonym: a word that means the same thing or almost the same thing as another word (for example, bawled, cried, wailed)

tense: the tense of a verb tells the time of the action, feeling, or state of being

verb: a word that expresses an action, feeling, or state of being

vivid verbs: strong, descriptive verbs

Bold numbers indicate Strategy boxes and Close-up pages.